The Existential Leader

The Existential Leader: An Authentic Leader for Our Uncertain Times invites us to reconsider our preconceptions about leadership, introducing a new model more in line with our uncertain times: existential leadership.

Monica Hanaway presents an illuminating overview of existential thinking and describes how an understanding of philosophy can improve leadership, drawing on existing leadership theories to show how this new model is more fitting for the challenges of today. The approach is primarily philosophical, rather than systemic or behavioural. It invites us to re-examine what we think about leaders, whether we really need leaders at all, and, if so, which existential concerns leaders must address. The book offers an introduction to the development of existential thinking and main concerns, including meaningfulness, anxiety, loneliness, freedom, choice and responsibility, authenticity, and values and beliefs. These are explored in the leadership context, with practical approaches for using these in everyday leadership dilemmas. Unique and accessible, *The Existential Leader* paves a way for modern leadership perfectly suited to the challenging times we live in.

Innovative, theoretical and applicable to our changing world landscape, this book will appeal to coaches, HR and L&D professionals, executives, business consultants, and current and future leaders. It will also be of interest to academics and students of coaching psychology, applied philosophy and psychology.

Monica Hanaway is an accredited mediator, psychotherapist, supervisor, leadership coach, management and leadership trainer. She designed the Middlesex University MA in Existential Coaching.

'In my work with leaders I am acutely aware of the challenges of today's world with all the uncertainties we face. I welcome a book which understands these existential leadership challenges and integrates wider philosophical ideas with the practicalities of the role of leader. The author explores the nature of leadership and the styles this takes, and introduces a new existential approach, which although embodying the ideas of existential philosophy, psychotherapy and coaching provides a practical grounding for leaders in the 21st century. This book is a resource for leaders and those working with leaders as trainers, coaches or consultants.'

– Colleen Harris MVO, FRSA, MICG; personal brand coach; communications adviser; diversity adviser; Deputy Lieutenant of Greater London, UK

'For anyone willing to embark on a healthy jog through the history of existentialist thought and phenomenology, Monica Hanaway translates this theory into a framework for action that has relevance for the choices to be made, not only by leaders, but by everyone involved in the life of an organisation. For those of us who find "the business of life" itself frequently challenging, what a comfort it is to find an author who can make this topic sing, in a genre too often associated with gloomy introspection. *The Existential Leader* is a practical, no nonsense & learned reflection on 'being' in the world - a book for anyone trying to better appreciate & better manage this human condition we find ourselves in.'

– Tim Macready, Executive Chairman & Founder of SKILL CAPITAL LLP

'Leadership has always been important, but the emphasis is changing. The hierarchical boss culture is no longer fit for purpose. The increasing pace of change and complexity means that leaders must adapt and modify their leadership style to inspire that "can't wait to get to work" ethos. Most effective leaders have one element in common – people want to work with them. Monica Hanaway's *The Existential Leader* sets out clearly the rationale for collaborative leadership and provides a well-illustrated approach for developing authentic leaders. This book is one that every leader should keep in their bookcase.'

– Felix Spender, former army officer, international negotiator and SME business leader

'As a leader and leadership trainer I am passionate about equipping leaders for the challenges of the world we live in. At this time of great uncertainty, we need a leadership approach which holds this uncomfortable truth at its core. In writing *The Existential Leader*, Monica Hanaway provides a practical leadership approach which embeds the existential concepts of uncertainty,

freedom and anxiety which all leaders face today. These philosophical concepts are presented in a clear, practical and straightforward way.'
- Yvonne Coghill CBE, OBE, FRCN; Professor of Primary Care and Head of Child Health at the School of Public Health, Imperial College London; Director at NHS Workforce Race Equality Standard (WRES) Implementation in NHS England. She is a member of the equality and diversity council at the Institute for Healthcare Improvement (IHI) in the United States

'As Chair of the Tutu Foundation UK (Patron Archbishop Desmond Tutu, Honorary Patron FW de Klerk), I grasp the extraordinary parallels between Existential Phenomenology and the African philosophy and tool of Ubuntu, lived and promulgated by Desmond Tutu and indeed Nelson Mandela. I have worked with Monica Hanaway in Belfast where she listened to the Leaders of the Loyalist Paramilitary who wanted somehow to move forward in their lives and help the next generation both as a whole group and then as smaller units. I was extremely impressed by her disciplined psychologically informed way without taking notes, without telling them what to do, without promising anything and could yet afterwards in private with me describe exactly what had been said and draw conclusions about where they were coming from as individuals. This approach is mirrored in *The Existential Leader* and there are lessons to be learnt for leaders in all contexts.'

– Clive Conway, Chair TFUK

'Monica Hanaway's book is unique in that she has managed to blend existentialism and leadership in practice in such a way that reader will not have to wade though treacle in order to grasp the philosophical concepts that underpin this approach to leadership. In other words, she uses the philosophy as an applied rather than an academic science. This is existential thinking in action in the context of being a leader. Having said that, this is a book that will be of interest to anyone who is interested in the dynamics of working with others while also being very thought provoking for readers who are interested in an existential and a psychological understanding of relationships.'

– Diana Mitchell, UKCP reg, psychotherapist, acc. mediator

The Existential Leader

An Authentic Leader for Our Uncertain Times

Monica Hanaway

First published 2019
by Routledge
2 Park Square, Milton Park, Abingdon, Oxon OX14 4RN

and by Routledge
52 Vanderbilt Avenue, New York, NY 10017

Routledge is an imprint of the Taylor & Francis Group, an informa business

© 2019 Monica Hanaway

The right of Monica Hanaway to be identified as author of this work has been asserted by her in accordance with sections 77 and 78 of the Copyright, Designs and Patents Act 1988.

All rights reserved. No part of this book may be reprinted or reproduced or utilised in any form or by any electronic, mechanical, or other means, now known or hereafter invented, including photocopying and recording, or in any information storage or retrieval system, without permission in writing from the publishers.

Trademark notice: Product or corporate names may be trademarks or registered trademarks, and are used only for identification and explanation without intent to infringe.

Monica Hanaway

British Library Cataloguing-in-Publication Data
A catalogue record for this book is available from the British Library

Library of Congress Cataloging-in-Publication Data
A catalog record has been requested for this book

ISBN: 978-0-367-02337-9 (hbk)
ISBN: 978-0-367-02338-6 (pbk)
ISBN: 978-0-429-40011-7 (ebk)

Typeset in Times New Roman
by Taylor & Francis Books

Contents

	List of illustrations	viii
	Acknowledgments	ix
	Foreword	x
	Introduction	xiv
1	What do we mean by 'existential'?	1
2	What do we mean by 'leadership'?	25
3	The twenty-first century leader	35
4	What do we mean by 'existential leader'?	48
5	Leadership in the context of existential concerns	52
6	Existential leadership skills	85
7	Four ages of existential leadership	104
8	Conclusion	118
	Bibliography	121
	Index	126

Illustrations

Figures

0.1	Existential continuum	xv
1.1	Existential dimensions	22
5.1	Overlap of existential dimensions and Reiss motivating values	78
6.1	Existential dimensions in organisations	102
7.1	Paradoxes in worldview	107

Table

6.1	Emotional intelligence domains and competences linked to existential issues	98

Acknowledgements

I am fortunate to meet so many interesting and inspiring people along my journey. Those who mean a lot to me know who they are and how grateful I am for what they give me.

However, there are some very special people I wish to thank. First of all, I need to thank my wonderful husband who puts up with my passions and my disappointments with equal acceptance. Without his steadfast support, and selfless encouragement, I would be unable to pursue my enthusiasms. He gives me the confidence to be me. Many thanks for being who you are, and having the patience to listen to and read various versions of this text as it developed.

I feel proud of my two greatest achievements (accomplished with a little help from my husband) - bringing two exceptional, creative, brilliant, and caring young women into the world.

I wish to thank my eldest daughter Cleo. Dr Cleo Hanaway-Oakley, to give her full title. She is the real academic in the family and encouraged me to put my thoughts in writing and to submit the original proposal for this book. Without her this book would never exist.

The other special person in my life is my younger daughter, Pascha. She constantly makes me smile, keeps me amused, encourages me to be creative, and can lift my spirits and reenergise me. Without her unflagging support and belief in me many of my projects would not have seen the light of day.

I must also thank my dear friends Diana and Allan Mitchell who graciously allowed me to use one of their son Duncan Mitchell's beautiful paintings for the book cover. I feel the image reflects the existential leader bravely stepping forward with the balloon of hope amidst the surrounding uncertainty.

I also wish to thank Laurence Colbert for his scholarly support when most needed.

I am fortunate enough to have all these people in my life and I would also like to take the opportunity to celebrate the life of my friend, colleague and co-mediator, Paul Randolph. Sadly Paul will never get the opportunity to read this book as he lost his fight with cancer on 8th January 2019. I am sure we would have had some interesting discussions. Paul, you are missed.

Foreword

We are living through quickly changing and uncertain times. As Dylan warned in the 1960s, times are 'a'changin' and indeed times are always changing. We never stand still, yet how many of us would have thought that we would have Donald Trump elected in the States and a vote for Brexit here in the UK? My parents lived through changing times, having survived the Second World War, but once rationing was over and they were both back in work and building a home and a family I believe that they thought and hoped that nothing much would change from then on. When I consider their lives, very little did change for them in the world of work. My mother worked for the same company the whole of her working life. She took time off to have my brother and myself and then returned to the same job but working part- instead of full-time. My father worked his way up in the same factory he started at as a sixteen-year-old, moving from the factory floor to production manager. He then did have to face a major change when the factory changed hands and he was made redundant, but within months he was back in the same post but in a different company.

When I first started work I believe I had an expectation that I would find a post I would stay in 'for life'. Having obtained a degree in Fine Art, I did one of the few things the degree qualified you for – became a teacher. I shan't bore you with my CV, which, although it makes little sense to others, to my mind followed a meaningful, if somewhat circuitous path. Although I did stay in one organisation for many years (indeed too many), it was in a number of different posts, chosen to fit my values and passions … or so I thought. I am now lucky enough to be one of those people who can undertake what is generally known as 'portfolio' working. I can take my interests, knowledge and skills and use them in a number of challenging contexts. I work as a leadership coach and trainer with individuals and organisations, and also work as an existential psychotherapist, and in conflict situations as a mediator. In all these roles I draw my inspiration from existential and phenomenological thought.

Moving on a generation, my younger daughter works in the film industry. She works 24/7 when she has a contract for a specific film. Between these contracts she seeks out any temporary work she can get, approaching each new challenge as a potential script writing opportunity, drawing on her temporary work colleagues for inspiration. My elder daughter is an academic, a very old profession; yet even here the nature of the work has changed considerably with extra administration and the stress of REF (Research Excellence Framework) demands requiring a specific number of articles, conference papers or books per year and the growing tension in universities to operate as businesses, in addition to being centres for research and teaching.

The change in our working patterns calls for a change in how we approach and give meaning to work, and in turn this challenges leaders to find a new and appropriate way of leading. As work takes up more of our time, is less certain and we are likely to change jobs more often, I believe that leaders have to find ways of making the working experience more meaningful for themselves and for those they are leading.

Of the large number of people, coming from different backgrounds and interests, who are beginning to question what it takes to be a leader who is appropriately responding to the needs of today's society, there seems to be an agreement that finding 'meaning' is essential in the exploration of a new leadership model. Porras, Emery and Thompson (2007) devote much of their research to the place of meaning in business success. My own approach to making meaning is quite similar to theirs, which I shall refer to throughout this book, but comes from the influence of existential and phenomenological approaches which I believe have much to offer to leadership.

Most books about existentialism and phenomenology sit on the shelves amongst philosophy books, often gathering dust, focused on thinking rather than doing. I have no desire to lose myself in philosophical thought, no matter how interesting I may find it. I wish to bring philosophy into action in daily living and into a sphere from which it has often, in my own experience, seemed sadly lacking – the world of business.

One way of introducing a more philosophical approach is through the training of leaders, as they can be seen to hold the most potential influence in changing the ethos of the world of business. A number of writers have looked at the influential aspects of leadership. Child (1972) developed the 'Upper Echelons Theory' which considers influence and decision making in relation to strategic leadership. The essence of the theory is that when leaders are required to make decisions in complex and ambiguous situations, they make those decisions based on very existential elements, that is, on their own values, beliefs and behavioural inclination (Canella & Monroe 1997, Finkelstein & Hambrick 1996, Hitt & Tyler 1991). The organisations from which these leaders come will in turn reflect the emotions, cognitions and values of those leaders. As we shall see, these determinants are the very stuff of existential being.

Interest in the existential approach is increasing. A growing number of people are exploring ways in which the lessons learnt from the approach can be applied in a practical way to the world of business, whether or not the debt to existential thought is overtly acknowledged (e.g. Lipman-Blumen 2000,

Visser 2008). This now takes the approach beyond the academic setting and places it firmly in the life, organisational, and business arenas.

I have always been keen to use an existential approach in my own leadership positions and when I left one leadership post I was keen to explore ways the approach could be introduced more widely. So, in 2010, I approached Emmy van Deurzen at the New School of Psychotherapy and Counselling, London, to see if she might be interested in offering training in existential coaching. Emmy had established the school on the foundation of existential thought but the training offered focused on existential psychotherapy. I wanted to build on this and take a more business accessible approach. The initial dialogue led to the development of a new MA in Existential Coaching which is now validated through Middlesex University.

In addition to training I was looking for other ways to extend the message and so in 2011 I worked with others on writing the first book which focused specifically on Existential Coaching – *Existential Perspectives in Coaching* (van Deurzen & Hanaway 2012). This book explored the philosophy underpinning the approach and contrasted and compared it with other approaches. The contributing authors' chapters aimed to look at what an existential approach brought to their coaching practice. The book did not focus on the skills used in the approach so in 2014, with Jamie Reed, I wrote *Existential Coaching Skills: The Handbook* (Hanaway & Reed 2014), which began to address this need. Students who competed the MA and readers of the books have begun to take the existential ideas into their work with business leaders. Established coaches have also begun to take an interest in the approach as a different way of working and thus adding a new offering to their portfolio of services.

In my psychotherapy work, I often work with leaders who are well known for their great commercial success. To the outside world they are undoubtedly successful in the terms in which the dictionary defines success. Such definitions are usually focused on 'achieving an aim', 'impressive achievement especially of fame, wealth or power'. They tend not to consider meaning, happiness, engagement or the like. Porras, Emery and Thompson (2007) consider the current definitions to be 'a potentially toxic prescription for your life and work … that makes you feel more like a failure than a success if it is the standard against which all meaning in your life is measured'. Many of my 'successful' clients are seeking something richer than these common definitions and seek a definition which includes aims such as 'living meaningfully', 'making a difference', 'empowering others', 'creating lasting and meaningful change'. Having achieved wealth, power and in some cases fame, these clients find they need more in order to consider themselves to be a success. They remain keen not to rest on their laurels but to continue to ask themselves fundamental questions around their self-concept and identity – Who am I? What are my values? What is my purpose? How do I exist meaningfully in this uncertain world? How do I find meaning in my life and in my work? How do I remain excited and stimulated by my leadership? These are all existential questions.

As a coach I work individually with many leaders and potential leaders who are showing increasing interest in learning more about existential thought and its practical relevance to leadership. They wish to frame a model of leadership which places existential concerns at its core. Several have been keen to introduce the approach to their whole organisation and so invited me to work within their organisations to offer in-house training in existential leadership to their leadership and management teams. Their aim is that it will become the presenting ethos of the organisation through which it demonstrates its values and beliefs, through the use of models of ways of working with the existential concerns of freedom, power, uncertainty and meaning.

I have continued to carry out research and to develop a specifically existential approach to leadership. This research and my reflections form the framework for my courses and presentations, but recently people have asked if there is a book in which they could find most of these ideas drawn together. Not considering myself to be a writer, I started writing this book to address their request as I could find no other book solely dedicated to the existential leadership approach. During the writing of the book I have come across others undertaking research around aspects of the subject (e.g. Agapitou & Bourantas 2017) and it is good to see the increasing interest for those looking to improve how we manage and lead.

This book is not intended to provide a comprehensive text on existentialism, or even existential leadership but to act as an introduction to the subject and exploration of what it is which makes a leader existential. As an investigated discipline, existential leadership is in its infancy. I hope this book acts as an invitation to you, the reader, to become involved in the development and practice of a new model of leadership.

If you are in the business world I invite you to take a look at your work context and ask yourself a number of questions – How can I be an existential leader? Can I demonstrate a more connective and authentic approach? Can my leadership be more meaningful for myself, and those who experience it? In other words, can I be more of an existential leader?

If you are not in business you will no doubt be a leader in other areas of your life, within which the approach is equally relevant. I hope I am able to start the reflective process with you by adding some theory, but perhaps more importantly, by posing some questions that you can ask yourself, and for which only you will have the answers.

Whatever has brought you to this book, I hope you find it interesting, clear and stimulating.

Introduction

People new to existential thinking tend to link it to images of dark jazz clubs, the pungent smell of Gitanes cigarettes, whisky, coffee, amphetamines and sleeping pills, and a bleak, nihilistic and selfish approach to life. Even worse, it may be seen as relating to arrogance, and possibly racist and Nazi beliefs. It is often the case that these associations have been formed before actually reading anything existential. These beliefs can cause people to attempt to steer clear of what is perceived as potentially depressing, even dangerous, literature. However, once they really take a look at what existential writers have to say, they may find that things can be seen very differently. The particular emphasis on temporality and time, with its constant reminders that life is short and we all shall die, may seem negative or defeatist but can also be seen as a clarion call to give each minute of life the importance due to something so fleeting. If we can do this, the world may take on a sharper and more interesting flavour. Indeed, we may find a world which is both more exciting, and more challenging due to its temporality, and where the need to consider and take responsibility for our own individual actions becomes paramount. I shall expand on these basic existential thoughts throughout this book.

The way one interprets existential thought will, quite rightly, be down to the individual. Several authors (van Dusen 1957, Patterson & Watkins 1996, Yalom 1980, Visser 2008) have explored the line within existential thinking which places 'pessimism – darkness and death' at one end and 'optimism – light & life' at the other (Patterson & Watkins 1996). (See Figure 0.1.)

A similar exploration has taken place with regard to Sartre's (1966) 'non-being' and Marcel's (1958) 'being' and the stance taken by Christian and atheist existentialists. The importance of our freedom to choose what we are is characteristic of all existentialist thinkers. Although I feel at this point, I should state that Marcel did not enjoy being regarded as an existentialist and indeed, in writing in 1950 in his *Metaphysical Journal*, he declared, 'The term existentialism brought with it the worst of misunderstandings and I now consider I have repudiated it once and for all.' He preferred to identify himself as a Neo-Socratic thinker, removing skepticism from his thinking. Despite having no formal religious upbringing or early strong religious beliefs, Marcel

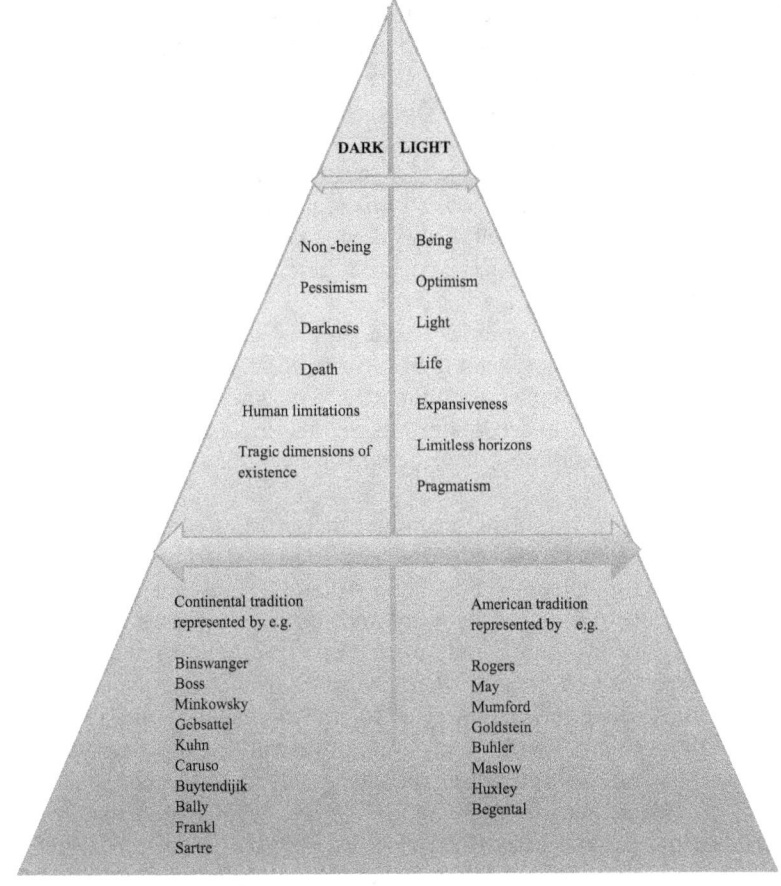

Figure 0.1 Existential continuum
Adapted from Visser (2008), van Dusen (1957), Patterson & Watkins (1996), Hanaway & Reed (2014)

recognised early on that his thoughts were leading him in a religious direction and in 1929 at the age of thirty he converted to Roman Catholicism. On his baptism on March 23rd he noted, 'I was baptised this morning. My inward state was more than I had dared to hope for: no transports, but peaceful, balanced, and full of hope and faith'. The importance of hope is evident in all Marcel's 'existential' thinking.

This Christian take on existentialism followed on from the work of the nineteenth century Danish philosopher and theologian, Søren Kierkegaard, with the emphasis on the need for doctrine to be derived from human experience whilst rejecting any appeal to eternal essence. Indeed, both Christian and atheist existentialists believe that human beings are forced to create themselves. Marcel's Christianity informs his existential perspective and belief that the existential life is largely one of hope, although not one of optimism. For Marcel, being in the world as body provides us with the opportunity to seek out new experiences and possibilities for the self. Marcel's hope is deeply pragmatic, in that it refuses to compute all of the possibilities against oneself. It is not faith that things will go well, because most often, things don't. Yet, even if there is despair in our situation, he believed there is always movement towards something more. If there is always movement, and always more to reach for, the existential self is never complete. The mystery of being for the existential self is unsolvable, because it is not a problem to be solved, but an experience to be reflected on, and explored, and ultimately to be worked toward. Experiences change, society evolves, and relations emerge, the individual who seeks meaning through an investigation of their being will never be fully satisfied and will remain in flux.

Sartre approached his thinking from his atheism. Along with Nietzsche he is well known for his much quoted statement 'God is dead', and his view that existentialism was a humanism bringing a vision of a brave, new godless world. If we cannot look to God for certainty and direction we must form our own values and ways of living in a finite world. Life has no meaning a priori. Sartre's decision to take God out of the equation did not come from an unwillingness to engage with the possibility of God's existence; Sartre was intimately familiar with theological debates concerning free will and the determinisms, or in theological terms, sin and grace. He was a student of Descartes and Malebranche, as well as Jansen, Pascal and Fénelon. That one of the twentieth century's most notorious atheists should have engaged to such an extent with theology may be a surprise. Sartre's (1966) atheist philosophy, as expressed in Being and Nothingness, involved a rejection of a particular kind of Christian theism, but the role theology played in the formation of his philosophy has not had due consideration. Although referring to God as dead, he also refers to God as being 'absent' and as 'an old flame', referring in *Words* to 'the atheist' as 'a man with a phobia about God who saw his absence everywhere and who could not open his mouth without saying his name' (Sartre 2000, p. 62). The atheist existentialist has to live with the 'absurdness' of life which ends in death and the ontological insecurity that creates.

Despite these somewhat academic considerations, the existential approach is an eminently practical and 'common sense' approach which focuses on our experience of living in the world as something we cannot partake in without other people. This renders the approach essentially relational in its understanding of 'being', thus meaning that the approach cannot be inherently selfish – I am concerned with how I am and how I act in relation to others. Some people may consider, like Sartre, that 'hell is other people', whilst others may consider the thought of being without others to be unbearable. It is that need for others which can at times feel equally hellish. Whatever our stance, our being is in response to others – how we choose to behave in relation to that knowledge is individual ... we can't live with them and yet we can't live without them! Even if we choose to cut ourselves off from all human interaction, we can only do this because there are others to cut ourselves off from.

To understand and accept our own agency in the decisions we make and to understand that we always have some choice in events, even if only in how we choose to perceive them, presents a challenge on how we choose to live life. We cannot look to causal explanations for our behaviour or the limitations we put on our own potentiality. We understand that there are limitations; as an individual I am 'thrown' (Heidegger 1962) into the world into a complex context – nationality, culture, family, race etc. I may 'fall' into a background of poverty or wealth or be blessed with a strong and healthy body or one with inherent weaknesses. I haven't chosen these circumstances but I do choose how to live with them and respond to them. I saw this forcefully demonstrated when I attended the Paralympic Games in London in 2012 where those competing were not deterred by their physical circumstances.

You may be wondering how all these ideas fit within the field of leadership. We do not tend to equate the world of philosophy with that of business and leadership. However, just like philosophy, leadership has also become a subject of academic interest. Many books have been written on styles and traits of leadership, and there are many websites, books and courses aimed at developing leadership skills. It is not my aim to focus here on these types of system and skill led leadership, but to consider the meaning of leadership and how as a leader one can focus on making working life meaningful for yourself and those you 'lead'.

Just as life is essentially relational, in that we are always living in relation to others, the same is obviously true in leadership. A leader cannot exist without a follower. Each follower will bring their own set of values, beliefs and meaning into their relationship with the leader. If we understand and work with this, we are beginning to approach leadership in an existential manner.

Although in this book I have structured my thinking about the development of an existential leader mainly within the business context, it is important to remember that there are many spheres of our life outside of the workplace where we take on, or relate to leadership. We are all leaders and we are all followers.

Chapter 1

What do we mean by 'existential'?

If we are to develop an understanding of existential leadership, we need firstly to understand what we mean by the terms 'existential' and 'leadership'. Let us start by exploring what we mean by 'existential'.

Marcel first coined the term 'existentialism' (*l'existentialisme*) in the early 1940s as a way of describing the thoughts of his friends Jean-Paul Sartre and Simone de Beauvoir. There was a precedent for the term in the German philosopher Karl Jaspers' idea of 'Existenzphilosophie', as well as Martin Heidegger's idea that when it comes to the kind of beings we are, our essence lies in our existence. Indeed, even earlier, Socrates showed a deep concern with the self and self-knowledge, so the roots of existentialism can be seen in the very early stages of western philosophy.

Today we will regularly see or hear the word 'existential' scattered around the media in connection with all manner of things. Currently, it would seem the world is governed by existential angst and we are in the midst of endless existential crises. Generally, the word is being used to imply something mysterious, complex, profound or sometimes even just trendy or cool. However we understand it in the media field, we should perhaps accept that even existential scholars are not in full agreement as to what constitutes existentialism.

This is quite fitting, as existentialism emphasises the unique perspective each of us brings to our experience of the world. As Spinelli (2005) described it, we live in 'an interpreted world' in which we come to our own conclusions about the meaning we choose to give things. Despite the growing common usage of the word, what can we understand by the term 'existential'?

The British philosopher Gary Cox (2009) in his book *How to Be an Existentialist: or How to Get Real, Get a Grip and Stop Making Excuses* offers us a useful definition to start our own exploration of what existentialism is, 'Existentialism is all about freedom and personal choice. It is all about facing up to reality with honesty and courage and seeing things through to the end, as well as being about putting words like choice in italics.' He warns that it requires effort to sustain the approach, believing that most people will want you to succumb to what existentialists call 'bad faith' or in Cox's words, 'Bad faith is a lot like what serious artists, musicians and rock stars call "selling out"'.

Essentially, existentialism is about the human condition and calls on each of us to live honestly, or as existentialists would term it, authentically, from a starting point of life having no meaning other than the one we choose to give it. It focuses on the belief that inner conflict within a person is due to that individual's confrontation with the givens of existence – the inevitability of death, freedom and its attendant responsibility, existential isolation, and meaninglessness.

Existential thinkers and writers have focused on different aspects of the philosophy and are not always in agreement. Nor would some of them accept the label of 'existentialist' in relation to themselves. Having them round the same dinner party table would certainly produce an interesting evening. I shall just give a brief overview of the approach of a few key 'existential' thinkers so we can begin to identify some common interests.

A brief overview

Overall, the core philosophy of existentialism can be described as being concerned with the 'problem of existence'. This has been seen as a product of the twentieth century, with its characteristic themes of interest in alienation, angst, absurdity and preoccupation. However, it has much earlier beginnings and it derives directly from Kierkegaard, who was born almost a century before Sartre.

Kierkegaard (1813–55) was ahead of his time. He brought about a long-overdue reexamination of one of the first philosophical questions ever to be asked: 'What is existence?' Kierkegaard insisted that every individual should not only ask this question but should make his very life his own subjective answer to it. He believed that Christian beliefs and the 'objectivity' of science were being misused to avoid the anxiety of human existence. He called for people to be courageous and take the leap of faith and live with passion and commitment from the inward depth of an uncertain existence. In Kierkegaard's view, this purely subjective entity lay beyond the reach of reason, logic, philosophical systems, theology, or even 'the pretences of psychology'.

Nietzsche (1844–1900) is known for his statement that God is dead. He saw the idea of God as outmoded and limiting and believed that we must re-evaluate existence in light of this. He challenged people to accept the reality of free will and to take responsibility for their choices, introducing the important existential themes of freedom, choice, responsibility and courage.

Thinkers like Kierkegaard and Nietzsche looked to Husserl's phenomenology (Husserl 2009) for a method to address and explore these themes. Husserl proposed a whole new mode of investigation and understanding of the world and our experience of it. Prejudice and assumptions needed to be put aside or 'bracketed', in order for us to meet the world afresh and discover what is absolutely fundamental and only directly available to us through intuition. If people want to grasp the essence of things, instead of explaining and analyzing them, they have to learn to describe and understand them.

Heidegger (1889–1976) applied this phenomenological method to understanding the meaning of being (Heidegger 1962). He argued that deep philosophical thinking rather than scientific knowledge can bring greater insight into what it means to be human in the world. The importance of time, space, death and human relatedness lies at the heart of his thinking. He favoured hermeneutics, an old philosophical method of investigation, which is the art of interpretation. Unlike interpretation as practised in psychoanalysis (which consists of referring a person's experience to a pre-established theoretical framework) this kind of interpretation seeks to understand how the person themself subjectively experiences something.

Sartre (1905–80) contributed many other strands of existential exploration, particularly in terms of emotions, imagination, and the person's place in a social and political world. Existentialists suggest that it is possible for people to face the anxieties of life head-on and embrace the human condition of aloneness, to revel in the freedom to choose and take full responsibility for their choices. They aim to have the courage to be. This does not mean ignoring the feelings of meaninglessness, but choosing new meanings for their lives.

Practical use of existential thought

At the beginning at the twentieth century we begin to see some psychotherapists inspired by phenomenology and existential thought. They sought to explore the possibilities of using this thinking in working with people. Often cited as early existential therapists, Otto Rank, an Austrian psychoanalyst, and Ludwig Binswanger, a psychiatrist at the Kreuzlingen sanatorium, attempted to bring existential insights to their work with patients. Binswanger's work inspired others such as Paul and Rollo May, who played an important role in developing existential therapy in America.

Further development took place in Europe, with the development of a method of existential analysis by Medard Boss in close co-operation with Heidegger, and with Viktor Frankl's development of logotherapy, an existential therapy which focused on finding meaning. In France, Sartre, Merleau-Ponty and others further developed existential ideas.

Medard Boss (1963, 1994) developed Daseinsanalysis, a form of psychotherapy which united the psychotherapeutic practice of psychoanalysis with the existential-phenomenological philosophy of Heidegger. In this, existence is open to any and all experience, we are alone with ourselves. It focused on concepts of personhood, mortality and the paradox of being alone yet living in relationship to others.

As mentioned earlier, Viktor Frankl (2003), an Austrian neurologist and psychiatrist and importantly a Holocaust survivor founded 'logotherapy', a form of existential analysis. He contributed enormously to our exploration of meaning and the essential role it plays in man's existence. His experience in a concentration camp led him to believe that even in the most brutal circumstances man will seek out a meaning to make the experience bearable. He identified three psychological reactions experienced by all prisoners to one degree or another: shock during the initial admission phase to the camp, apathy after becoming accustomed to camp existence, in which the inmate values only that which helps himself and his friends survive, and reactions of depersonalisation, moral deformity, bitterness and disillusionment if he survives and is liberated. Frankl concludes that the meaning of life is in every moment of living; life never ceases to have meaning, even in suffering and death. He believed that for everyone in a dire condition there is someone looking down, a friend, family member, or even God, who would expect not to be disappointed. Thus a prisoner's psychological reactions are not solely the result of the conditions of his life, but also of the freedom of choice he always has, even in severe suffering.

Merleau-Ponty (2013) focused on the embodied nature of our existence, that our understanding of the world comes via the body and its relationship with mind. I am sure we have all experienced our thoughts and emotions through our body. We can feel sick with excitement, blushes may accompany shame, our legs may tremble with fear etc. There is an emphasis on first-person activities and subjectivity, with the body generating its own consciousness. Merleau-Ponty also believed time and temporality to be subjective. Our memories of the past, and our hopes for the future, are not based on facts, but on our interpretation of the events past and future. Taking his interest in perception into the arena of freedom, he saw 'total freedom' as limited by our perception of obstacles to that freedom.

Sartre's ideas found fertile ground in Britain. R. D. Laing and David Cooper, often associated with the anti-psychiatry movement, placed his ideas centrally in their work (Laing 1960, 1961; Cooper 2007; Laing and Cooper 1971). They used them as the starting point by which to critically reconsider the notion of mental illness and its treatment. They founded the Philadelphia Association, an organisation drawing on the studies of Wittgenstein, Levinas, Foucault and Lacan to provide alternative living, therapy and therapeutic training. Perhaps their most famous project was Kingsley Hall, in London, where patients lived through their 'madness' without the usual medical treatment.

The existential approach in Britain was further developed through the establishment of a number of existentially based courses in academic institutions. This started with the programmes created by Emmy van Deurzen, initially at Antioch University in London and subsequently at Regent's College, London (now Regent's University, London) and then at the New School of Psychotherapy and Counselling (NSPC), London. I was fortunate to study at Regent's during a very exciting time for existential thought, when both Emmy van Deurzen and Ernesto Spinelli were members of the teaching faculty. Ernesto Spinelli has worked to demystify therapy and to develop existential thought in the areas of coaching and business consultancy. Freddie Strasser, with whom I was also fortunate enough to work, developed an existential approach to time limited psychotherapy and brought existential thinking and a psychological approach into the alternative dispute resolution (ADR) arena.

Some core ideas in existential philosophy

Existential thought talks a lot about 'Being' (by which we mean all human experience). As already alluded to, the approach concentrates on our experience of 'Being' in the world on a temporal journey – how we experience our life and how we approach the decisions we have to make. Although we are unique and will each experience our lives differently, there are a number of things we all share, and which an existential approach posits, cannot be avoided. Yalom identifies these commonalities, or 'givens', as – death, freedom, responsibility, existential isolation and meaninglessness. Engaging with these givens is essential to pursuing an existential approach. Simplistically, it could be claimed that 'Being' is also underpinned by three core assumptions:

- **Relatedness:** We experience ourselves and everything around us – the World, other people, us included, in the context of a relationship.
- **Uncertainty:** This related way of experiencing reveals that 'Being', life, is uncertain –uncertain in its meaning, its future and because there exists no certainty beyond the finite nature of our existence and the uncertainty itself.
- **Anxiety:** This awareness produces an anxiety that is all pervading and never ending as long as we are alive.

Existential thinking focuses on issues relating to those assumptions – freedom, responsibility, authenticity, purpose, meaning, paradox, uncertainty, anxiety, values, time and temporality.

Everyone who exists in the world is free to change at any time. The world gives us no definitive meaning, we must find meaning ourselves. This brings with it a great deal of anxiety, as the freedom to choose and bring meaning to life brings with it responsibility which we cannot ignore. Whatever I decide is my decision, it is not forced on me. I have made a decision with the knowledge that for everything I say 'yes' to, there is a 'no' which is experienced as a loss.

It is true that we do not choose to be born into this world or in this time. This is termed 'thrownness'. We are thrown into an existence we did not choose. However, once here we are free to choose what we make of our lives. The responsibility we have for choosing to become what we are causes anxiety, and can lead to living authentically or inauthentically.

Of course, if we cannot look for external truths or theories, we must look to a deep exploration of the phenomenon of our experience, a discipline know as phenomenology, literally the study of the 'phenomena'. Phenomenology (from Greek *phainómenon* 'that which appears' and *lógos* 'study') is the philosophical study of the structures of experience and consciousness. As a philosophical movement it was founded in the early years of the twentieth century by Edmund Husserl (1859–1938) and was later expanded upon by a circle of his followers at the universities of Göttingen and Munich. It then spread to France, the United States, and elsewhere, often in contexts far removed from Husserl's early work.

As with existentialism, different authors share a common family resemblance, but have many significant differences, so a unique and final definition of phenomenology is dangerous and perhaps even paradoxical as it lacks a thematic focus. It is not a doctrine, nor a philosophical school, but rather a style of thought, a method, an open and ever-renewed experience having different results, and this may disorient anyone wishing to define its meaning.

Phenomenology, in Husserl's conception, is primarily concerned with the systematic reflection on, and study of, the structures of consciousness and the phenomena that appear in acts of consciousness. Phenomenology can be clearly differentiated from the Cartesian method of analysis which sees the world as objects, sets of objects and objects acting and reacting upon one another. Its object is to systematically describe a phenomenon from different angles and intuitively grasp its essence in a new way. So, everything we encounter, we interpret, we make assumptions about its meaning. The only things we can draw on to help our interpretation are our past experiences and knowledge. Unfortunately we often leap from interpretations to assumptions to beliefs and we act on those beliefs as though they were evidenced 'truths'.

A phenomenological approach gives us no 'truths' to fall back on. It requires us to 'bracket' all our assumptions and to focus on things as they appear in our experience, that is, on the way we experience things and the meaning we give to them – the significance of objects, events, tools, the flow of time, the self and others, as these things arise and are experienced in our 'life-world'.

Phenomenology studies conscious experience as experienced from the subjective or first person point of view. It concerns itself with thought, memory, imagination, emotion, desire, volition to bodily awareness and embodied action, and social activity, including linguistic activity. The structure of these forms of experience typically involves what Husserl called 'intentionality' – the directedness of experience toward things in the world, the property of consciousness that it is a consciousness of or about something. Phenomenologists base their understanding about how we exist in the world on the premise that humans interpret something so that things can be identified and have meaning, thus objects exist through the meaning that we give them. Every act of intentionality contains two parts: the noema and the noesis (Husserl 2009). Noema is directional, it is the object (the what) that we direct our attention towards and focus upon, the 'fact or content'. Noesis is referential, the 'how' through which we define an object. It is concerned with the individual's uniquely emotional and meaningful experience of that content. We must listen for and pay attention to both aspects. Everything is interpreted by the individual through the veils of their familial, cultural and individual experiences, including their value sets and emotional context.

Husserl's conception of phenomenology has been criticised and developed not only by himself, but also by students such as Edith Stein and Roman Ingarden, by hermeneutic philosophers such as Martin Heidegger, by existentialists, such as Nicolai Hartmann, Gabriel Marcel, Maurice Merleau-Ponty, Jean-Paul Sartre, and by other philosophers, such as Max Scheler, Paul Ricoeur, Jean-Luc Marion, Michel Henry, Emmanuel Levinas, Jacques Derrida, and sociologists Alfred Schütz and Eric Voegelin. It provides rich reading beyond the scope of this book.

Let's return to the three core assumptions and look briefly at each one.

Relatedness

Where does it all start? Whether we like it or not we live in this world with other people. Our very existence is relational. The existence of others is the source of our joy and our despair. We discover who we are by looking to others. I know I am female because I can encounter males and recognise the difference. I know I am not a child, nor elderly because I have access to both those groups and can see that although I may value their company, I do not *belong* in either.

As we grow up, our image of who we are is largely based on how our parents and others treat us. This is known as 'mirroring'. In the early years, the concept of mirroring involves a parent's reflection of a child's expressed thoughts and feelings. We begin to see ourselves through the eyes of our parents and to learn what they value and what aspects they seem to reject. If I cry for milk will my thirst be sated? If I cry out for company will someone come to me? If I share what is important to me, will I be listened to? Ideally those kinds of needs are met and we grow up to feel that we are accepted and loved, whether successful or not. For each of these needs to be met we need another person to respond to us.

As we grow, we internalise this validation and enter adult life with a realistic and workable degree of self-acceptance and self-awareness, enabling us, if our experience of being mirrored was positive, to start with a core belief that we are acceptable to others and thus able to participate in social functions. Throughout our life, this belief may be rocked by individual events and experiences, but overall we retain a sense of our right to exist.

However, if parents do not mirror a child authentically, a child may become self-absorbed in a compensatory effort to feel OK. Other children may struggle with an inability to identify and express an authentic self, frequently fabricating an identity in order to get approval from parents and peers.

It is not always easy for a parent to provide a good 'mirroring'. Parents can struggle to provide accurate reflections when they are trapped in their own battles with identity. Some parents find intimacy difficult or are so self-absorbed they are not able to see and reflect to their children accurately. The lack of mirroring can be subtle yet traumatic. It may lead to a sense of worthlessness, which a child may spend the rest of their lives accepting as truth, or may struggle to revise. It can be very confusing to the child when the parent is able to engage others with ease and with expressions of concern or understanding, and yet not appear to do the same for them.

We take this early self-concept with us. We come to see ourselves as being basically lovable or not, as having our expectations met, or not, and we begin to seek evidence from others to support or challenge that concept.

Existential thought starts with the belief that although humans are essentially alone in the world, they long to be connected to others. People want to have meaning in one another's lives, but ultimately they must come to realise that they cannot depend on others for validation, and with that realisation they finally acknowledge and understand that they are fundamentally alone (Yalom 1980). The result of this revelation is anxiety in the knowledge that our validation must come from within and not from others.

Throughout life our self-concept is challenged. People may seem to experience us in ways we don't understand or we feel that to succeed in a particular context we must change who we consider ourselves to be. In order to live effectively in the world we need to relate to others both in a personal and professional capacity.

Our need for others to help us experience ourselves is not always positive. Other people can help us to understand ourselves better, they can respond positively to us and to our needs, yet equally they may obstruct us in achieving what we desire. Our relationship with others is therefore often paradoxical.

These kinds of dilemmas can be fundamental and embedded, and the basis for a reflective exploration, or they can be contextual and boundaried, needing to be explored in the context of one event or for a specific purpose.

Uncertainty

The concept of uncertainty is one with which many of us struggle and which lies at the heart of death anxiety – we know we will die, but we do not know how or when, we have no certainty about what, if anything, happens to our 'being' after death. However, uncertainty is also a challenge in life. We can never be certain how things will work out, how long things will last and what challenges we may be faced with. The philosopher, author and journalist Albert Camus (1913–1960) sees the hopeless human desire to make sense of our condition and to establish certainty where it does not exist, as being essentially absurd and impossible. He challenges us to respond appropriately to this situation and to live in full consciousness of our state of uncertainty and absurdity.

If we accept this truth, Camus posits that three consequences follow – 'revolt, freedom and passion'. By 'revolt' he means defiance with this absurd truth, experiencing it as not hopeless but life giving in its essential temporality. Through recognising and accepting the absurdity we can liberate ourselves from habit and convention, bringing about a 'passion' to live intensely, not to escape the sense of absurdity but to face it with absolute lucidity. Kierkegaard (2009, p. 515) responds to the absence of certainty and the need for passion by stating, 'I must find a truth that is true for me ... the idea for which I can live or die.'

For some people, it is this uncertainty which makes life full and exciting. If we really knew everything that would happen before it occurred, where would that leave us? Would we enjoy the challenge if we always knew the outcome? Would we embark on creative activity if we could be sure of the end product? Auguste de Villiers de l'Isle-Adam (2000, p. 62) wrote, 'Uncertainty is a quality to be cherished ... if not for it, who would dare to undertake anything?'

However, many people seek certainty, yet as David Levithan (2011, p. 4) writes, 'The mistake is thinking that there can be an antidote to the uncertainty.' He acknowledges it as terrifying, yet also inviting, 'in the way as an artist may face a blank canvas, or a writer, a clean sheet of paper ... Anything can happen, it may be beautiful or it may be ugly but it will "be"'.

We try to avoid this uncertainty in a number of ways. Some people attempt to use positive thinking, which Karen Cerulo (2006) calls 'optimistic bias' which may include an element of self-delusion, making it harder to face uncertainty at those moments when it cannot be avoided. This may leave us unprepared for real threats.

Others may choose to focus on smaller things in order to be distracted from and avoid the bigger question of uncertainty. O'Gorman (2016) suggests that, 'worrying is also an attempt to control the unknown. Worrying is, among other things, a "futures management technique" ... That is to say, worrying is an attempt to assert some authority over what is ahead and, however modestly, to arrange it to our benefit.'

Anxiety

It is certainly the case that for many of us it is life's uncertainty which leads to anxiety. We cannot control even our own lives. We did not decide the date or nature of our birth, nor can we do so for our own death. Even in suicide there lies uncertainty – will it work, will I feel pain, will people grieve, will I have any consciousness beyond my last breath?

Heidegger (1962) points to the ontological origin of existential anxiety as 'Being-towards-the-end'. Its presence is not seen as pathological, but a natural response to the nature of existence. Van Deurzen (1997) sees the presence of existential anxiety as a call to re-examine life and address its meaning and purpose. Likewise, Spinelli (2007) notes that existential anxiety is not avoidable as it is present in 'all reflective experiences of relatedness' (Spinelli 2007, p. 21). It is a 'given' of human existence; 'the dilemma of existential anxiety is not so much that it is, but rather how each of us "lives with" it.' When we embrace it, it still remains with us. If we reject it, it causes more anxiety. In including anxiety in our life, Kierkegaard writes, 'Whoever has learned to be anxious in the right way has learned the ultimate' (Hannay & Marino 1998, p. 324). We need to be fully aware of the positive challenges which anxiety presents, whilst also acknowledging the struggle which we experience when faced with our anxieties.

Existential concerns

In addition to the 'core' assumptions, there are a number of other, interlinked existential concerns, within which the core assumptions operate:

- Emotions – including existential guilt and existential anxiety
- Values, beliefs and meaning
- Freedom, responsibility, facticity and choice
- Sedimented beliefs, action patterns and values
- Time and mortality
- Authenticity

As a consequence of these and the three basic core assumptions we are free and as such are forced to find ways of keeping at bay the anxiety that freedom brings. One way in which we seek to do this is to develop 'coping strategies'. For these to work they have to be imbued with meaning which reflects our values and forms our sense of Being. We may be born (thrown) into a family and community with very strongly defined and held values. We may choose to embrace these values or to disown them and take an opposing view. I was once shocked when a colleague was filling in a form and stopped to ask 'What religion am I?' answering his own question with 'Well I guess I am Church of England, as that's what my parents are.' Even this demonstrates a choice, a choice not to engage with his own beliefs but to choose to adopt those of his parents, perhaps without even knowing what they were.

Through the creation of meaning, either adopted or self-formed, we seek to appease anxiety and find a frame of reference for understanding our lives. This is termed our 'worldview', encompassing how we see the world, ourselves and others in it, and the meaning we give to things. It is a view which is always seen through the 'lens' of our values and beliefs and thus provides us with individualised, subjective meaning to protect us from the gaping anxiety caused by the deep uncertainty that pervades all our lives and is revealed to us in the context of relatedness.

Now that we have a way of seeing the world, a framework for understanding it and giving it meaning, we can, and indeed must, make choices, not just about our values and beliefs, but also about what we want to do with our lives and how we want to behave. We can ultimately decide how we want to define our lives.

The level of choice we enjoy goes deeper than this. Because we have chosen our values and beliefs, we can potentially change these values whenever we choose. In doing so we can change how we see everything, that is, the way we see ourselves, what we have done, how we see ourselves now and how we see ourselves being in the future.

Unfortunately, changing our worldview, values and beliefs, isn't that straightforward as it requires us to confront the underlying anxiety and uncertainty. However, it is possible for people to face the anxieties of life head-on and embrace the human condition of aloneness, to revel in the freedom to choose and take full responsibility for their choices. They can courageously take the helm of their lives and steer in whatever direction they choose; they have the courage to be.

Camus' (2013) novel, *L'Etranger*, provides a good example. The main character, Meursault, accepts his mortality and rejects the constrictions of society, leaving him unencumbered and free to live his life with an unclouded mind. Camus acknowledges the existential anxiety which is caused, yet challenges us to respond and live in full consciousness of our state of uncertainty and absurdity, and embrace the truths of temporality and freedom. Soren Kierkegaard also places the responsibility for how we rise to these challenges firmly on the shoulders of the individual. For both, it is up to us to find our own meaning or project through which we can experience passion and probably pain.

Let us look a little more closely at the core concerns I listed earlier: Emotions – including existential guilt and existential anxiety; Values, Beliefs and Meaning; Freedom, Responsibility, Facticity and Choice; Sedimented Beliefs, Action Patterns and Values; Time and Mortality and Authenticity.

Emotions

The Latin root word 'mot' means 'move' as in motivation, remote, and emotion. Motion is nothing but 'moving' of some kind. Our emotions are not static, they wax and wane, emotions shift and flux. As the original French word *émouvoir*, meaning 'stir up', implies they do indeed stir *us* up. Emotion is any conscious experience characterised by intense mental activity and a high degree of pleasure or displeasure. Emotion is often intertwined with mood, temperament, personality, disposition and motivation. In some theories, cognition is regarded as an important aspect of emotion. Those acting primarily on the emotions they are feeling may seem as if they are not thinking, but mental processes are still essential, particularly in the interpretation of events. For example, the realisation of our believing that we are in a dangerous situation and the subsequent arousal of our body's nervous system (rapid heartbeat and breathing, sweating, muscle tension) is integral to the experience of our feeling afraid. Other theories, however, claim that emotion is separate from and can precede cognition.

Existentialists believe that our human 'essence' or 'nature' (way of being in the world) is simply our 'existence' (being in the world). Existentialism is often connected with what are often considered to be *negative* emotions, such as anxiety (worrying), dread (a very strong fear) and mortality (awareness of our own death). As a group willing to express these aspects of being, existentialists are deeply interested in emotions.

The interest is not just in emotions themselves, but also, just as Blake points out in 'The Grey Monk', emotions tell us something. They are 'intellectual' and as powerful as a 'sword' (Blake 2002, p. 105). We are never emotional about nothing but always in response to and about something. In phenomenology this is termed 'intentionality'. Emotions inform us about ourselves and about others. They direct us towards what is important enough to 'stir' us and thus inform us about our values, beliefs and assumptions regarding one's self, others, the world and the cosmos.

Phenomenology focused more than most schools of thought on the nature and meaning of emotions and brought the study of emotions to the forefront of philosophical inquiry. It might be thought that phenomenologists focus on emotions because the felt quality of most emotional states renders them a privileged object of inquiry into the phenomenal properties of human experience. This might lead one to think that phenomenologists attend to emotional experience for its highly subjective character. On the contrary, it is the ability of emotions to engage with reality that makes them crucial for phenomenological analysis. Emotional experience is an opening to the salient features of a situation; undergoing an emotion is a way, perhaps the principal way, in which the world manifests itself to us. The theories of Sartre and Heidegger flow from a view of emotions as explored by Brentano, Husserl and Scheler and further developed by Merleau-Ponty, Levinas and Ricoeur. Robert Solomon has brought phenomenological theories to current agendas.

Heidegger considered that through experience we are somehow attuned to the world; that moods are prior to emotions; that we are always in some mood and that there is a small set of fundamental moods attendance to which reveals important truths about human existence. Emotions are always present in ourselves and others. Even the quietest person sitting immobile in the corner will be experiencing an emotion. How the same emotion is manifested externally, through our bodies, may look quite different in different people.

I remember a day many years ago, my first day on a Masters course. I was one of eighteen students starting that day. I felt very nervous and this emotion intensified as the day progressed. As the lecturer began to speak, other students would enter into dialogue with him, particularly one student, Zelda, who when we had all introduced ourselves reported that she already had a Masters in the History of Ideas. Just knowing that she had already successfully completed a Masters course frightened me ... was I good enough to be doing this course? ... had they sent me the wrong letter? ... should it have been a rejection rather than an acceptance? For the next few hours Zelda continued to joust with the lecturer showing a huge knowledge of a subject which was very new to me. As the day progressed a tight band seemed to constrict my head, I felt sick. As a result I said nothing and stayed as still as possible trying not to draw any attention to myself. Over the years Zelda and I became friends. One day we were reminiscing about that first day and I was shocked to hear how she had experienced me. 'You were so confident, you didn't feel you had to prove yourself, you sat there very zen, confident in your own skin, whilst I frantically searched my memory for any information I could shout out which would demonstrate my right to be there.' What a revelation, we were both struggling with very similar emotions yet we manifested them very differently and as a result misread one another and made ourselves feel lacking in comparison.

If I don't assume I know how the other person is feeling, I can explore it with them and through their emotions. I can discover their worldview and in doing so, as Heidegger pointed out, I discover important truths about human existence.

Freddie Strasser, a past mentor of mine, used to tell of the psychotherapy client who sought therapy because he was unemotional. 'Help me to feel emotion,' he requested. Wisely Freddie replied, 'What do you feel about not experiencing emotions?' and the client answered with a string of emotions: 'I feel weird, different, insecure, worried...' It seemed there was no further work for Freddie to do, the unemotional client had discovered his emotions!

Of course, emotions are complex things. We can experience more than one emotion at the same time. I may be feeling happy because I am in the company of friends and enjoying food and wine and at the same time feeling guilty that I have left my home in a mess, which my partner will come back to. Rather like the lens on an old single lens reflex camera those feelings will fluctuate. First one will be in the foreground and then it will move to the background, constantly shifting as we focus on different things.

We also have emotional responses to emotions. We have emotions about emotions – I can be angry at my new puppy because she distracts me from my work and wants to play, while at the same time I can feel guilty because she is only being a puppy and at another time I would be delighted to play with her.

Ratcliffe (2008) identified that in addition to emotions there are 'existential feelings'. Existential feelings constitute, to use Ratcliffe's words, 'how we find ourselves in the world', in general. In contrast to emotions and emotional episodes Ratcliffe believes existential feelings manifest a different type of intentionality: they are not directed towards anything specific; rather, they are background orientations through which everything we perceive, feel, think and act upon is structured. Whereas one might be angry about something specific, such as being insulted, a mood is directed at a more encompassing state of affairs, perhaps even the world as a whole.

Values, beliefs and meaning

As human beings we share an existential given – a belief that humans seek and need meaning. Living with meaninglessness generates existential angst. Sartre, as an atheist, rejected the idea that there is a divine meaning to one's life or that there is a purpose for which each individual is born. In *The Myth of Sisyphus*, Camus (2000) introduced the notion of absurdity which arises from the clash between the world's resounding silence (meaninglessness) and the individual's expectation of purpose or direction. Heidegger, in *Being and Time*, maintained that the realisation of this meaninglessness leads to a feeling of Angst. He maintains that Angst is not specifically focused on what is impacting on any one individual, in the present moment, but is concerned with the bigger picture – the world, and indeed the cosmos itself. Human existence is not only 'being-in-the-world', in the here and now, but also our 'potentiality-for-being' and of course, the inevitability of our future non-being.

Even in the most challenging circumstances, such as Frankl's concentration camp experiences, man seeks meaning, shaped through values and beliefs. Our need to do this is one of the human givens we share and which defines our humanity. How we do it differs for each individual. Some people look to institutions like religion, political parties or cults to provide them with structured meaning; others will seek to find it on an individual basis.

Our behaviour is governed by our values and beliefs. I may do something because I believe it is the right thing to do, or I may choose to do the opposite, despite believing it to be wrong. Whatever the choice of behaviour, it will be in relation to a value being enacted or ignored. When my own values are attacked, my meaning is also under attack. I experience myself as being under threat and in conflict, with all that this raises for me.

Freedom, responsibility, facticity and choice

Philosophers have pondered the notion of freedom for years. From Thucydides, through to Thomas Hobbes, John Locke, John Stuart Mill and Jean Jacques Rousseau, the concept of freedom has continually been dealt with to some degree in philosophical and political thought. This is an important concept because we must decide whether individuals are free, whether they should be free, what this means and what kinds of institutions, including businesses, we wish to build around these ideas. Freedom is one of the most significant themes examined by existentialists and a major cause of existential anxiety.

Sartre gives a complex and compelling account of existentialist freedom as a 'doctrine of action' (Sartre 1966), which pushes man to find himself again. For Sartre, the intention of existentialism 'is not in the least that of plunging men into despair' but to allow them to realise themselves as 'truly human'. He believes that all of us are always free to choose and thus responsible for our actions and must 'therefore choose'. He uses the example of being in a war – in times of war, it may seem that many of the conscripted soldiers have no freedom as they are forced to fight but the truth is that they do have choices. They could run away from their country, or commit suicide. The reason they end up fighting in the war is because they considered the consequences of each of their options and decided that fighting was the best choice. As such, they freely chose and are responsible for being in the war.

Of course there are times where we are not free. We do not ask to be born, nor can we decide the family or circumstances we are born into ('thrownness'/ '*Geworfenheit*'). We may not have been in control in 'deciding' to exist, but we are in complete control of our existence. Facticity is another term for this concept. Sartre defines the concept as 'in-itself' both a limitation and a condition of freedom. It is a limitation in that a large part of one's facticity consists of things one couldn't have chosen (birthplace, etc.), but a condition of freedom in the sense that one's values most likely depend on it. However, even though one's facticity is 'set in stone' (as being in the past, for instance), it cannot determine you as a person: the value ascribed to one's facticity is still ascribed to it freely by that person. As an example, consider two men, one of whom has no memory of his past and the other who remembers everything. They both have committed many crimes, but the first man, knowing nothing about this, leads a rather normal life while the second man, feeling trapped by his own past, continues a life of crime, blaming his own past for 'trapping' him in this life. My coaching and psychotherapy clients often talk of this sense of being 'trapped', yet we are never totally or truly trapped. We can take agency of what brought us to that situation and of the possibilities and potentialities for freeing us from it. Unfortunately, the resulting freedom can sometimes seem as unattractive as the 'trappedness'.

Like it or not, we are responsible for making our own decisions. Indeed, to *not make* a decision is *to make* a decision, in that we have *decided* not to decide. If we have responsibility for ourselves, and there is no definitive authority, then we are forced to embrace the existential twins of freedom and angst. Nietzsche in *The Gay Science* and in *Thus Spoke Zarathustra*, repeatedly declares that God is dead, that he does not exist, or even that he did, but no longer exists. He suggests that God could be considered a dream, which we needed to help us cope with the fact that life is just space and time between two points. Nietzsche suggests that when we stopped needing god we 'killed him' (Nietzsche 2006, p. 81). However, as Nietzsche acknowledges, even if we have 'killed' God we find it difficult to free ourselves of God's shadow: 'After Buddha was dead people showed his shadow for centuries afterwards in a cave, – an immense frightful shadow. God is dead: but as the human race is constituted, there will perhaps be caves for millenniums yet, in which people will show his shadow' (p. 108). It is down to us to make that time meaningful. Without the existence of God, there is no pretense of our lives being mapped out according to some grand divine plan. How our life turns out is purely our own doing, not because of any external forces beyond our control. As such we must formulate for ourselves what is 'right' and what is 'wrong'. We decide our own morality.

Without the existence of god, there is no pretence of our lives being mapped out according to some grand divine plan. How our life turns out is purely our own doing, not because of any external forces beyond our control. As such we must formulate for ourselves what is 'right' and what is 'wrong'. We decide our own morality.

Positive freedom is 'positive' in the sense that individuals will want to be their own master by virtue of positive freedom. Berlin (1969) believed that one will 'wish to be a subject, not an object' and so will pursue an ideal of 'true liberty' in order to achieve full human potential and thus live virtuously. In his essay, Berlin (1969) claims that 'conceptions of freedom directly derive from views of what constitutes a self' (Ralston 2011, p. 94).

In existential freedom one may change one's values, as one is responsible for them regardless of society's values. The focus on freedom in existentialism is related to the limits of the responsibility one bears as a result of one's freedom: the relationship between freedom and responsibility is one of interdependency, and a clarification of freedom also clarifies that for which one is responsible.

Man is free when his consciousness acknowledges that something is lacking, when he makes a purpose of himself, and when he commits. In Sartre's words, this is when he 'transcends' himself. Every action is a commitment.

To be free is not comfortable because freedom creates anxiety and anguish, individuals may flee in self-deception and continue leading inauthentic lives. Even when we choose to do nothing, we are making a choice. Everyone who exists in the world is free to change at any time. The world gives no meaning, we must find meaning ourselves. In this uncertainty the freedom to choose and bring meaning to life brings with it a responsibility intimately entwined with anxiety/angst.

Sedimented beliefs, action patterns and values

Our beliefs, values and behaviours provide us with meaning and a baseline from which to consider our actions. Over time we find that certain actions or behaviours seem to work for us and be consistent with our value system. Unfortunately we can become stuck in these behaviours which no longer work, without recognising that they have become a habit. These can become what existential-phenomenological theory terms 'sedimented'. If you think of the dregs of coffee left in the bottom of a percolator, the dregs do not shift by a simple shake, one needs to put in some work to clear them away – it is possible, but not easy.

Sedimented beliefs, then, are those that insist on the primacy, or correctness, of one particular perspective over all others. However limited or irrational they may be, it will take a great deal to override their interpretative power. Spinelli (2005) sees sedimented beliefs as the foundational 'building blocks' of our constructed self. It must be recognised that however restrictive, all sedimented beliefs serve to define the self-construct, create a feeling of stability and security, guard against uncertainty, and as such, challenging them may be met with fear and resistance.

We are divided beings not only in terms of the dissonance between our beliefs and experiences concerning our self-construct, but, just as importantly, in terms of our desire to break down the sedimented beliefs that have given rise to this dissonance and the opposing desire to retain these beliefs. Stated simply, we want to change, yet remain essentially the same. One cannot change 'bits' of the sedimented self-construct without its effects being felt by the whole, as it alters the entire structure.

We often feel at our most emotional when our values are attacked. The attack may come from others or ourselves (when we find ourselves in 'bad faith' behaving in ways which go against our beliefs). By understanding this, we can identify emotional stressors. A too rigid (or sedimented) adherence to a value may be problematic; for example, if an individual places 'loyalty' high in their value set they may feel the need to follow the behaviours of their peers or institution even when they experience those behaviours as destructive or wrong.

Time and mortality

One of the existential challenges we all face is the willingness to embrace that our time on earth is limited – we shall all die. This can sound a bit like the voice of doom but is in fact a challenge to embrace the temporality and to fully live in the moments we have.

When we consider 'death' we must remember that we are considering not just the reality of physical death and the move towards it which comes with the aging process, but we are also considering various layers of symbolic death. No human being can constantly hold the awareness of death. Becker (1973) points out that such awareness would be too overwhelming and potentially drive people to neurosis or psychosis.

This may all be sounding a little dark and deep when we are considering business leadership. However, throughout life we suffer a lot of small deaths – death of hope, future, confidence, the ending of a relationship, job or course. Each of these experiences brings us in touch with our feelings about death and mortality. For the existentialist it is vital to work to create a healthy balance between an awareness of death/loss and the propensity to become overwhelmed and terrified by it.

For some people the fear of death and the need to leave something behind means that they strive hard in life to create a legacy as a form of immortality. Otto Rank (2011) believed that some people seek to be heroic so that the rules of death no longer apply to them and Becker suggests that Freud's investment in the development of psychoanalysis was his way to overcome death by creating something which would live beyond him, so that at least his memory would never die. In many cultures the ancestor only truly dies when people stop remembering them.

Yalom (1980) is another existential writer who has given consideration to our responses to the reality of death. He postulated that there are two ways of denying death: either by becoming a rescuer or through being special. Many comic book heroes and god-like figures of mythology serve to save people from death. If we spend our time saving others we do not have to think of our own inevitable demise. We see this theme every day, with managers focusing on their staff whilst failing to recognise the vulnerability and temporality of their own position.

For those who adopt Yalom's 'specialness' they hold the belief that they have something so special about them that they cannot 'die'. When they are faced with the evidence that this is not true, for example, through redundancy or illness, they are shocked and ill-equipped to deal with the change.

Many people deny the reality of death by avoiding living, in a vain attempt to stay safe. They may avoid investing in relationships for fear of being hurt, rejected or abandoned. They go through life terrified of living because of their deep terror of death. To contemplate death means contemplating our human limitations. One of the most powerful limitations we face is 'not knowing'.

As humans we want to know. We speak of 'knowledge as power'. This is not a bad thing in itself; it leads to new explorations, learning, discoveries and new inventions. The negative aspect lies in the false belief that we can know and therefore control everything, that is, that reality can be fully known and secondly that it can be controlled. For many people it is the realisation that they cannot control everything which causes distress.

People tend to be afraid of the abstract and unknown, so they seek structure and a reified reality. Tillich (1952), writes of the tremendous courage required to live life in the face of anxiety and death. In order to experience the true beauty of life one has to become vulnerable to death and anxiety. We often hear those who are terminally ill speak of the new intensity of colour, smell and touch they experience when they accept their temporality. Acknowledging our vulnerable mortality can be experienced as not hopeless, but giving life, in its essential temporality, a certain grandeur. Through recognising and accepting the absurdity of our selves we can become free from habit and convention and see a liberating freshness, creating the passion to live as intensely as possible, not just to escape the sense of absurdity, but to face it with absolute lucidity.

Authenticity

Authenticity means genuine, original, not a fake (Concise Oxford English Dictionary, Eleventh Edition). It has roots in the Greek philosophy, 'To thine own self be true' (Harter 2002). Authenticity and sincerity have been used interchangeably, while there is difference between the two, as Lionel Trilling (1972, p. 4) defines sincerity as follows: 'Sincerity is congruence between avowal and actual feelings. While, authenticity is the extent to which one is true to the self'.

One's sincerity is to represent oneself to others accurately and honestly. Being true to others is sincerity, while being true to oneself is authenticity, one's relationship with one's self (Erickson 1995 and Trilling 1972). Harter (2002) writes of authenticity as the combining of one's personal experiences (values, thoughts, emotions and beliefs), and acting in accordance with one's true self (expressing what one really thinks, believes and behaving accordingly). Kernis (2003) defines authenticity as 'The unobstructed operations of one's true or core self in one's daily enterprise', identifying four components – awareness, un-biased processing, action and relational.

'Awareness' is in relation to our motives, feelings, desires and self-relevant cognitions and includes being aware of, though not limited by, our strengths and weaknesses, traits and emotions. By 'un-biased processing' he means not denying, distorting or ignoring internal experiences and external information. Our 'action' and behaviour must be authentic and in tune with our true self, beliefs and values as with the rest of our existence. Authenticity is therefore relational.

Existential philosophy places considerable importance on acting authentically despite external pressures. The centrality of authenticity is shown in the works of existential thinkers and writers such as Kierkegaard, Heidegger, Nietzsche and Sartre. It governs our engagement with ourselves, others, the world and beyond. In other words, it is related to our *being* rather than being a characteristic or property. Indeed, our *being* governs our doing. If we are working, indeed living/being existentially, we must do this authentically. This is easier said than done. We have all encountered times in life when we feel the pressure to appear to be a certain kind of person, adopt a particular mode of living, or ignore one's own moral and aesthetic objections in order to have a more comfortable existence – 'to fit in'. We can note this, acknowledge this or choose to ignore it and live in what existentialists may term 'bad faith'.

For Sartre, the 'vertiginous' experience of the recognition of our freedom and choices can feel so unbearable that some people choose to live inauthentically or, as Sartre would describe it, live 'in bad faith', rather than engage with life. People often stay in situations where they feel inauthentic due to fear of the uncertainty of tackling a more real and possibly precarious existence. We may stay in a relationship because we fear being alone rather than feeling an authentic love or commitment to the other; we may stay in a job that doesn't match our values and where we feel uncomfortable because we can't give up the security the job offers us. I am not saying that these decisions are bad, but to be authentic they must be acknowledged for what they are.

Kierkegaard focuses more on a belief that authenticity is reliant on an individual finding authentic faith and becoming true to oneself. Although a Christian, he developed the idea that the media and church-led Christianity present challenges for an individual trying to live authentically. He saw the media as supporting a society that does not form its own opinions but utilises the opinions constructed by the news. For him, organised religion is a tradition that is passively accepted by individuals, without authentic thought. Kierkegaard's idea of authentic faith is of an act which requires a turning from logic and experienced 'reality', and taking a *leap* of faith, which can be achieved by still facing reality, yet making a choice to believe, and once that choice is made, then passionately sticking with it.

As an atheist, Nietzsche (1960) rejects the role of religion in finding authenticity, calling for a finding of truth without relying on virtues or conventional morality. Thus the individual must stand alone and take responsibility for actively shaping his own beliefs. For Nietzsche the authentic man is someone who transcends the limits of conventional morality in an attempt to decide for himself about good and evil. He rejects the idea of religious virtues due to the lack of questioning by the individual and warns us to avoid what he calls 'herding animal morality'. The commonality of Kierkegaard's and Nietzsche's existential philosophies is the responsibilities they place on the individual to take an active part in the shaping of one's beliefs and then to be willing to act on that belief.

For Heidegger (1962), authenticity equated to *'mine-ness' (Eigentlich)* which is the idea that we not only 'have' but 'are' possibility, that 'we can own ourselves, or seem to do so, or we can lose ourselves, or never own ourselves, all based on how we each individually define our own "who am I"' (Mandic 2012, p. 24). This belief calls us to challenge any illusion we hold that we are defined by circumstances, culture, gender, family etc.

Some more recent writers, such as Erich Fromm (2001), do not call for the rejection of behaviour which is in accord with societal mores, if it results from personal understanding and approval of its drives and origins, rather than a desire for conformity and acceptance. Fromm considers authenticity to be a positive outcome of informed motivation rather than a negative rejection of the expectations of others. He described Sartre's 'absolute freedom' as 'the illusion of individuality', as opposed to the genuine individuality that results from authentic living.

Authenticity is a difficult state to achieve, due in part to social pressures to live inauthentically, and in part due to a person's own character. It has been described as a revelatory state, where one perceives oneself, others and sometimes even things, in a radically new way. It requires self-knowledge. It is the reflection of one's inner values and beliefs reflected in one's behaviour. It may be good or bad.

Erickson (1995) and Heidegger (1962) speak of the 'level' of authenticity in a person, as people are never entirely authentic or inauthentic but rather they seek to achieve a level of authenticity. We have the potential to become authentic but may need help in realising our potential. Authentic people are the most committed people to their goals and there is no need to motivate them (May et al. 2003).

Remaining authentic is not an easy task. Heidegger, in *Being and Time* wrote of the way in which we tend to fall under the sway of 'the they' (*das Man*), an impersonal entity that takes away our freedom to think independently. To live authentically requires us to resist and outwit this influence but this is hard as *das Man* is so nebulous. *Das Man* is not a separate entity, it is 'me', it is everywhere and nowhere. If we allow *das Man* to take responsibility for important decisions, it takes personal responsibility away. As Arendt (1998) says, we slip into banality, failing to think. We must find a way to tap into our 'voice of conscience': the authentic self, and wake up to our Being. This may result in setting us aside from everyone else. It may feel very lonely to be at peace with our own truth and to act accordingly.

To live authentically may be uncomfortable but what about the alternative, to live inauthentically, or as Sartre would describe it, to live in 'bad faith' (*mauvaise foi*)? To describe this Sartre offers the story of the Parisian waiter. This waiter is able to balance his tray 'putting it in a perpetually unstable, perpetually broken equilibrium which he perpetually re-establishes by a light movement of the arm and hand'. He moves beautifully but robotically. Sartre sees he is playing a game; he is playing at being a waiter in a café! We know what playing at a waiter requires. In G.K. Chesterton's tale 'Queer Feet', Father Brown is able to move between playing the part of a waiter and playing the part of a club member in a gentleman's club. We all have times when we choose to play a part, or more than one part. In business this often happens when people move through the hierarchy, taking on the perceived characteristics of each role – worker, boss, leader etc.

Sartre would consider that we are in bad faith when we portray ourselves through the prisms of our class, job, race, gender, culture, history, family and early influences, be they conscious or unconscious. To turn it on its head, living in good faith requires me not to make excuses and to take responsibility for my thoughts and actions.

The four existential dimensions

Another way of exploring these existential themes is through the framework of the four existential dimensions.

Whilst remaining a grounded, authentic and secure individual we all know that we do not always feel the same, or act the same in all contexts. We will choose to share different aspects of ourselves with different people. We may feel confident about singing and dancing at a party, yet would not choose to do so in the workplace. We will choose with whom to share our most intimate thoughts and desires and identify those with whom we will just skim the surface.

The 'givens' provide tensions and paradoxes which the individual encounters within the four dimensions of human existence; the physical/*Umwelt*, social/*Mitwelt*, personal/*Eigenwelt* and spiritual/*Uberwelt* realms. The core aspects, introduced above, can be found in all dimensions – relatedness, uncertainty and anxiety. We may identify one or more dimensions which are undeveloped. Once identified, the individual may seek to change the balance or just to note it and take responsibility for change or no change.

Figure 1.1 shows the four core dimensions in which we operate. The arrows in the diagram seek to remind us that the degree to which each dimension is prominent will vary over time. Some dimensions will be fully and richly inhabited at one time whilst others may appear quite barren.

Physical dimension

The physical dimension (*Umwelt*) is concerned with response to environment and the natural world around us. This includes attitudes to the body, to the surroundings, landscape, climate, objects and material possessions, our bodies and bodily needs, health and illness and mortality. The struggle in this dimension is between the search for domination over the elements and natural

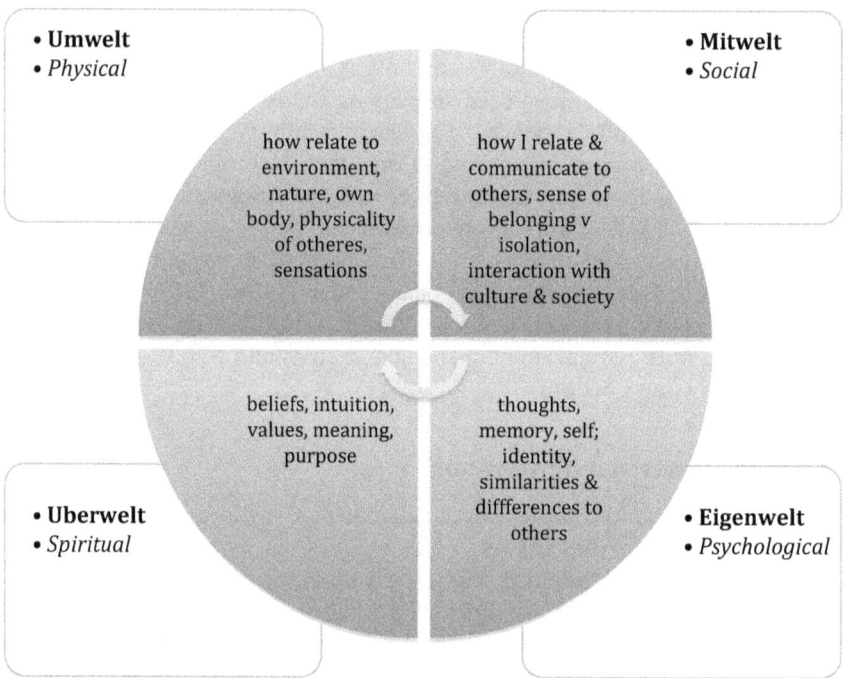

Figure 1.1 Existential dimensions
Hanaway & Reed (2014)

law (as in technology, or in sports) and the need to accept the limitations of natural boundaries (as in ecology or old age). While people generally aim for security in this dimension (through health and wealth), much of life brings a gradual disillusionment and realisation that such security can only be temporary. Recognising limitations can bring great release of tension.

Social dimension

In the social dimension (*Mitwelt*), individuals relate to others in the public world around them. This includes their response to the culture they live in, and the class and race they belong to (and also those they do not belong to). Attitudes may range from love to hate, from cooperation to competition. The dynamic contradictions can be understood in terms of acceptance versus rejection, or belonging versus isolation.

Some people prefer to withdraw from the world of others as much as possible. Others blindly chase public acceptance by going along with the rules and fashions of the moment or try to rise above these by becoming trendsetters themselves. By acquiring fame or other forms of power, individuals can attain dominance over others temporarily. Sooner or later, however, everyone is confronted with both failure and aloneness.

Psychological dimension

On the psychological dimension (*Eigenwelt*), individuals relate to themselves and in this way create a personal world. This includes views about their own character, past experience and future possibilities. Contradictions here are often experienced in terms of personal strengths and weaknesses. People search for a sense of identity, a feeling of being substantial and having a self. Inevitably many events will confront them with evidence to the contrary and plunge them into a state of confusion or disintegration.

Activity and passivity are an important polarity here. Self-affirmation and resolution go with the former, and surrender and yielding with the latter. Facing the final dissolution of self that comes with personal loss and the facing of death might bring anxiety and confusion to many who have not yet given up their sense of self-importance.

Spiritual dimension

On the spiritual dimension (*Überwelt*) (van Deurzen-Smith 1984), individuals relate to the unknown and create a sense of an ideal world, an ideology and a philosophical outlook. It is here that they find meaning by putting all the pieces of the puzzle together. For some people this is done by adhering to a religion or other prescriptive worldview, for others it is about discovering or attributing meaning in a more secular or personal way.

The contradictions contained in this dimension are often related to the tension between purpose and absurdity, hope and despair. People create their values in search of something that matters enough to live or die for, something that may even have ultimate and universal validity. Usually the aim is the conquest of a soul, or something that will substantially surpass mortality (as for instance in having contributed something valuable to humankind). Facing the void and the possibility of nothingness are the indispensable counterparts of this quest for the eternal.

Through reflection on these existential dimensions, and acceptance and consideration of the existential givens, a leader can develop a good understanding of the sense of 'being' carried by each individual they work with – how they are in the world and how they relate to it, in all its complexity. From the above we have identified what we mean by 'existential' and how its concepts fit into everyday existence. Let us move on to take a look at what this contributes to our understanding of 'leadership'.

Chapter 2

What do we mean by 'leadership'?

How is leadership defined?

As Lipman-Blumen (2000, p. 325) warned, 'the ongoing excavation of the leadership concept is part of a deeper search for the meaning of life, a search for how each of us mere mortals fits into the larger picture.' Definitions and understanding of leadership vary. Each gives emphasis to a particular aspect of leadership. Perhaps the simplest, and my favourite, is that given by Peter Drucker (1996) when he reminded us that the only definition of a leader is that every leader has to have followers, and that it is only by virtue of this followership that there is such a thing as leadership. Once a leader loses their followers they can no longer be a leader. Others, such as the leadership theorist Warren Bennis, focused on the leaders' ability to turn a vision into a reality, whilst Bill Gates prioritised the leader's ability to empower others and John Maxwell (2018), whilst listing 21 irrefutable laws of leadership, saw leadership as being nothing more nor less than the ability to influence people and things. Each of these tells us as much about the author as it does about leadership.

Why do we have leaders?

We must start with asking ourselves a question which is rarely asked – why have leaders at all? The concept of leader seems a universal one although different societies value different characteristics in their leaders. There seem to be few examples of leaderless action although there is a strategy of 'leaderless resistance, or phantom cell structure', a social resistance strategy in which small, independent groups, including individuals, challenge an established institution such as a law, economic system, social order, government, et cetera. While it lacks a central command, the concept includes a common goal between the individual actor and the group or social movement from which the ideology was learned. Even if there appears to be no named or material leader, if we look closely, there is usually a symbolic figurehead who sets objectives and identifies targets. This may not be a living breathing person but could be a written or verbal doctrine.

So if it is so common for societies to confer leadership on a person, what purpose is leadership serving? Sandling (2015) suggests that we are simply born with a natural desire to be led, guided, nurtured and supported throughout our lives in all situations.

I should like to place some of these elements in relation to our predisposed need for leadership within an existential context. We look to leaders to help us with the fundamental existential dilemma of finding meaning.

Followers confer leadership. We need someone/something to follow. Our first leaders are our parental figures. We tend to believe that if we follow their lead we will survive. This is a defense against uncertainty and gives me a project, 'survival', through which I can find meaning. It is all part of that fundamental question 'Why am I here?' Although this is a deep metaphysical and philosophical question it is part of our every breathing moment, constantly interrupting us as we go about daily life. We look to leaders to provide an answer to this question. Religious people will look to follow a religious leader but for general day-to-day activities we turn to our colleagues and superiors. Leaders help us to identify, understand and refine our purpose. They help us to align our thoughts and clarify the reasons behind our work. Humans seek answers and understanding in everything they do and leaders go some way to support this need.

This existential questioning and need for meaning and certainty means that even in adulthood when we find ourselves in new and challenging circumstances we look for leads on how to engage with these new experiences. We seek guidance, support and leadership to minimise the threat of getting it wrong, humiliating ourselves or doing something which will impact negatively on our relationships or potentiality. In some ways, we look to a leader to act as our rescuer from these uncomfortable realities. Yalom (1980, p. 129) proposed that we look to either personal specialness or an ultimate rescuer to save us from uncertainty and ultimately from death and that if this fails we look outside ourselves. 'Some individuals discover their rescuer not in a supernatural being but in their earthly surroundings, either in a leader or in some higher cause.' However, as Yalom pointed out, overall the ultimate rescuer defense is less effective than the belief in personal specialness.

A second existential issue is that of freedom and responsibility. Leaders provide us with a perceived defense against our existential freedom. If there is someone 'above' me making the decisions, then I can live in denial of my own freedom to decide. It is the decision maker that carries the blame if things go wrong and they provide the perfect mechanism for absorbing any guilt. Leaders should look the part, strong and wise, and provide a human shield we can hide behind. In this way we invest them with the 'personal specialness' Yalom wrote of and which we see most clearly evidenced in charismatic leaders.

Leaders can offer us a model of what we can be but don't expect to achieve. We can celebrate with them when they succeed, we see ourselves as part of that success but we are equally willing to disassociate ourselves from them when things do not go well, even to condemn them or take pleasure in their failure. As followers we have the gift to confer leadership and the power to take it away.

Leaders act as a tool to fight off two existential demons: uncertainty and anxiety. At the core of our human condition lies the immutable reality that we can neither predict nor totally control our destiny (existential uncertainty) and this knowledge challenges our sense of mastery and efficiency and leads to deep-seated dread (existential anxiety).

Leadership can be seen as a way of dealing with the ultimate existential experience – death. We have five-year plans, we have action plans with timelines and milestones, these give us a sense of continued existence, and yet in addition to corporeal death we have constant small deaths to contend with even in the business arena, including the three Rs of restructuring, redundancy and retirement.

We seem willing to make a devil's bargain with leadership. Leaders give us a feeling of security and in return we choose subservience, agreement to play by their rules, potential frustration and boredom. We risk their dissatisfaction, being misunderstood, and being just one of many. The need for security must be a strong one for us to enter into such a bargain.

The bargain is not just one way. Although most leaders consider that the benefits outweigh the costs, it is as they say, 'lonely at the top'. It may look to followers as though leaders are free and have more power over uncertainty, yet leaders also need to protect themselves from their existential fears. They too are entrusting themselves to others (divine or human). If a leader loses his followers he is no longer a leader. He is dependent on market forces, the board etc. and his fate is consigned to a powerful, controlling institution with a group ideology and associated set of values and beliefs. Although a leader may interpret their leadership position as evidence that they really are in control of their destiny, this is never truly the case.

Our relationship with leadership is ambivalent. An appetite for power, together with enormous self-confidence, can lead to corruption, bullying and tyranny. An arbitrary and unpredictable leader can intensify, not relieve our existential anxiety. We want our leader to be strong but knowing their faults can reassure us. It allows us to draw a little closer to our ego ideals. Ultimately, leadership offers us a safety valve – leaders can be brought down if necessary. Like it or not, leadership is directly connected to existential needs.

Types of leader

Leaders come in all shapes and sizes. When leaders appear they are set apart from the crowd, are treated as different, usually as superior, to 'ordinary' people. So, what is it that makes them different and causes us to treat them as special? Is it something about them? Do they hold particular skills or characteristics? Or is it something about us? Could it be that we are born with a natural desire to be led, that we are predisposed to feel a need to be guided, nurtured and supported throughout our lives at all levels and in all situations?

There is no clear understanding of what distinguishes leaders from non-leaders and ... what distinguishes *effective* leaders from *ineffective* leaders (Bennis & Nanus 1997). The type of leadership needed is contextual or situational; a style of leadership which works well in one situation may not succeed in another. Leadership styles could be grouped under seven basic headings:

- Leaders who are born not made
- Leaders who focus on what they have to do, and are able to learn how to do it
- Leaders who lead in relation to context
- Leaders who employ archetypal behaviour patterns
- Leaders focused on their relationships with others, followership and issues of motivation
- Leaders who see their role as making a better world
- Leaders who aim to fulfil specific organisational needs or emphases.

Leadership styles may seem to be in opposition to one another: autocratic/democratic; task-oriented/relationship orientated; bureaucratic/laissez faire. One style of leadership may be better suited to a certain time or situation. I am not offering a compendium of leadership styles here, there are many good books out there which do, but it is worth taking a broad look at where existential leadership fits.

Simplistically, one could say that leadership styles span a continuum from autocratic to participative (Likert 1967). Within that spectrum Likert identified four main styles of leadership, in particular around decision-making and the degree to which people are involved in the decision.

Exploitive authoritative

The leader has a low concern for people and uses fear-based methods to achieve conformance. Communication is almost entirely downwards and the psychologically distant concerns of people are ignored.

Benevolent authoritative

When the leader adds concern for people to an authoritative position, a 'benevolent dictatorship' is formed. The leader uses rewards to encourage appropriate performance and listens more to concerns lower down the organisation, although what they hear is often rose-tinted, being limited to what their subordinates think that the boss wants to hear. Although there may be some delegation of decisions, almost all major decisions are still made centrally.

Consultative

The upward flow of information here is still cautious and rose-tinted to some degree, although the leader is making genuine efforts to listen carefully to ideas. Nevertheless, major decisions are still largely centrally made.

Participative

At this level, the leader makes maximum use of participative methods, engaging people lower down the organisation in decision-making. People across the organisation are psychologically closer together and work well together at all levels.

Authoritative, autocratic and transactional styles

Following the world wars, many leadership positions in business were filled by those who had held leadership positions in the military. In war, a leader is not looking for reflective behaviour on the battlefront. They are not seeking participation. They need their followers to trust them implicitly. The leader's command may well be a matter of life and death, the soldier does not have time to stop and consider or they risk being killed.

In these situations it makes sense to have a transactional, directive and autocratic style which involves the leader retaining all the power and leading by instruction. Employees will have little or no input in decision-making processes and will work completely under the direction of the leader. The leader will create the goals, set the targets, assign the job roles and drive performance. These are models based on the assumption that people are motivated by reward and punishment, that social systems work best with a clear chain of command, that people cede all authority to the manager and that the prime purpose of the 'subordinate' is to do what they are told. It requires the leader to provide clear structures and to use rewards and punishments (salaries, bonuses etc.) to ensure compliance with their commands.

This model of leadership worked when people were used to being in the forces but came under challenge in the post-war years and as you can imagine did not fit easily with the mores of the 1960s when independent thought and free action were being encouraged.

Transformative leader

In contrast to a transactional approach we have the transformative approach, which began in the late 1970s and it has had a large impact on the way modern leaders think and behave. As a model it sought to explain the unique connections between leaders and followers which can enhance business success. It goes beyond the focus on transactional rewards to deeper issues.

A transformative leader engages, supports and empowers their employees. The approach assumes that people will follow those who inspire them and that a person with vision and passion can achieve great things through injecting enthusiasm and energy. Transformative leaders aim to develop a vision which they believe in and which is in line with their personal and professional values and beliefs. Having done so they believe that people will buy into a radical vision. Taking the vision forward, some transformational leaders know the way and simply want others to follow them. Others do not have a ready strategy, but will happily lead the exploration of possible routes to the 'promised land'.

Agapitou and Bourantas (2017) saw the approach as closely aligned with the followers' existential need for meaning based on values. 'Transformational leaders provide a sense of purpose, an articulated future-orientated and inspirational vision based on values and beliefs'. Bennis and Nanus (1997, p. 31) outlined what they believe to be the essential qualities of an effective transformational leader: having a clear vision for the future, being a 'social architect' for their organisation, creating trust through consistency and clarity and having positive self-regard. Overall, transformational leaders are considered to use high levels of emotional intelligence, be charismatic and show exemplary standards of consistency and integrity.

Charismatic leader

The German sociologist Max Weber (1968) thought charismatic authority stemmed from the leader's 'mana' or divine gift of grace which compelled awe. Charismatic leaders tend to appear at times of great distress when a radical vision is needed to resolve a crisis.

Weber speaks of the followers' response to charismatic leaders as a devotion born of distress. Charismatic leaders can induce a sense of dissatisfaction in followers thus creating the conditions required for their ascension to power. Such leaders are very powerful and hold power they can wield for good or bad.

Both transactional and transformative leaders can provide examples of charismatic leadership. Charismatic leaders tend to hold a number of assumptions – grace and charm are all that is needed to create followers; self-belief is a fundamental need of leaders; people follow others whom they personally admire. Charismatic leaders rely on their ability to 'work the room', 'play the house', that is, pull all the strings and build an image of the group or company in which they themselves are central. They are usually very skilled communicators, verbally eloquent but also able to communicate to followers on a deep, emotional level. They are able to articulate a compelling or captivating vision and to arouse strong emotions in followers. The emphasis for them is on how they use their personality and charm (sometimes even physical attractiveness), how they communicate to followers and whether they are able to gain followers' trust to influence and persuade them to follow by using verbal and body language. They are often inspirational and have a high level of motivational skill, using their ability to inspire and motivate followers to perform at high levels and to be committed to the organisation. Conger and Kanungo (1998) describe five behavioural characteristics of charismatic leaders that indicate a more transformational viewpoint:

- Vision and articulation
- Sensitivity to the environment
- Sensitivity to member needs
- Personal risk taking
- Performing unconventional behaviour.

Musser (1987) notes that charismatic leaders seek to instil both commitment to ideological goals and also devotion to themselves. The extent to which either of these two goals is dominant depends on the underlying motivations and needs of the leader. Interestingly, only the followers expect the leader to display charisma. His entourage does not hold such expectations, they can tolerate the leader being human and flawed (Bailey 2001).

Quiet leader

Both transactional and transformative leaders can place themselves at the forefront in their management style but it is not essential to lead from the front. The 'quiet leader' is the antithesis of the classic charismatic leaders in that they base their success not on ego and force of character but on their thoughts and actions. Although they are strongly task-focused, they are neither bullies nor unnecessarily unkind and seek to persuade people through rational argument and a form of benevolent transactional leadership. The approach is based on the leader's assumption that their actions speak louder than their words. They believe people are motivated when given credit, rather than when the leader takes credit, and so ego and aggression are neither necessary nor constructive.

The concept of the quiet leader is not a modern invention. Lao Tzu (n.d.), in the classic Taoist text *Tao Te Ching*, discussed the same characteristic around 500 BC:

> The very highest is barely known by men, Then comes that which they know and love, Then that which is feared, Then that which is despised. He who does not trust enough will not be trusted. When actions are performed Without unnecessary speech, People say 'We did it!'

Here the highest form of leadership is virtually invisible.

Servant leader

Servant leadership is a subtle form of leadership. The term 'servant leader' was coined by Greenleaf (1977) at the very beginning of the 1970s. A servant leader's main focus will be on the growth and well-being of the people and communities they are associated with. This is based on the assumption that a leader has responsibility for others and towards society, and particularly those who are disadvantaged in some way. For servant leaders the best way to help others is to lead them, and through this, people served grow as individuals, becoming 'healthier, wiser, more autonomous and more likely themselves to become servants' (Greenleaf 2008, p. 27). They aim to share power, prioritise the needs of others before their own and support people to maximise their development and performance. It is a principled leadership approach and Greenleaf identified ten key qualities of servant leaders:

- Listening
- Empathy
- Healing
- Awareness
- Persuasion
- Conceptualisation
- Foresight
- Stewarding
- Commitment to the growth of people
- Building community.

Servant leadership has gained much praise over recent years with many top CEOs championing its effectiveness. By supporting employees to thrive and succeed the leader ensures they are inspired and enthused to work free from barriers and issues.

Leadership preferences

Different people and different circumstances favour different forms of leadership. Douglas McGregor (1968) proposed the X and Y theory in which he explored these different preferences. He observed a number of leaders and managers operating in their place of work and as a result concluded that every leader could be categorised as either an 'X' or a 'Y' leader. Theory X proposes that humans have an inherent dislike for work and will avoid it where possible. Similarly, most people prefer to be directed, try to avoid responsibility, have little ambition and are happy with security alone. An 'X Leader' will attempt to counter this dislike by controlling, directing, coercing, threatening and punishing employees in order to get them to work.

In contrast, theory Y proposes that humans have a natural desire to work and pursue challenging goals. If the situation is favourable, people will find work to be a source of satisfaction, fulfilment and enjoyment. When trusted and engaged, people have the ability to work productively and effectively in a self-controlled and self-directed manner.

Another way of grouping leadership approaches is the extent to which they are focused on 'task' or on 'people'. In the 1960s, Blake and Mouton (1994) developed a 'Managerial Grid' showing two axes, measuring Concern for People (y-axis) and Concern for Completing Task (x-axis). Through a series of questions about their leadership and management style, leaders were seen as primarily showing 'Concern for People' in which the focus was the needs of team members, their interests and areas of personal development, when deciding how best to accomplish a task, or 'Concern for Task' in which a leader emphasises concrete objectives, organisational efficiency and high productivity when deciding how best to accomplish a task. Whilst someone's position could be anywhere on the grid depending on the relative importance they attach to People and Task, the grid highlights five extremes on the grid – each of which is given a memorable name:

Impoverished management (concern for people = 1, concern for task = 1): This is a laissez-faire style; minimal effort on management; hoping to avoid blame for errors.
Country Club Management (concern for people = 9, concern for task = 1): This focuses on creating safe, comfortable working environment; minimal conflict.
Task Management (concern for people = 1, concern for task = 9): This is an autocratic style, consistent with McGregor Theory X. Workers have to complete tasks, nothing else.
Team Management (concern for people = 9, concern for task = 9): In this, staff are closely involved in decision making and feel valued; consistent with McGregor Theory Y.
Middle of the Road Management (concern for people = 5, concern for task = 5): Here compromises are made to achieve acceptable performance; thought to be the least effective management style.

The more task-orientated leader is concerned with outcomes and the work that is being performed. They are primarily goal-focused and work effectively towards predetermined objectives. Less focus is placed on the individuals and teams performing the work as long as the work is done on time and to the required standard. Task-orientated leaders will define the roles within a team, divide the work up amongst the team, establish processes and procedures and monitor progress in order to successfully achieve the task in hand. As a task-orientated leader would see it, products need to be made and the employees are there to make them. Services need to be delivered and the employees are there to deliver them. Little attention is given to the attitudes, feelings, views and values of the staff. This style of leadership believes that staff will be motivated through the collective achievement of goals and objectives.

The more relational focused leader focuses primarily on the people who perform the work and in supporting, motivating and developing individuals and teams. They aim to establish meaningful relationships with their staff and aim to use emotional connection to maximise staff performance. They seek to empathise with their staff and understand things from their point of view. Relationship-orientated leaders encourage effective teamwork and collaboration through enhanced relationships that exist between team members. Understanding the needs and requirements of each individual person is vital if relationship-orientated leadership is to be effective.

The above gives a very brief overview of key theories and definitions of different styles of leadership but I am sure we have all experienced some of the very common negative leadership styles:

- Post-hoc Management: *Always wise in hindsight and never to blame.*
- Micromanagement: *Controls every detail.*
- Seagull Management: *Flying in, pooping on you and flying off again.*
- Mushroom Management: *Drop them in the poo and keep them in the dark.*
- Kipper management: *Two-faced approach.*

Chapter 3

The twenty-first century leader

Why we need a new type of leadership in the twenty-first century

The nature and pattern of work have always changed and evolved. Each decade presents new challenges and opportunities. We have moved from the industrial age to the information age. Economic uncertainty, the digital explosion, dramatic changes in customer and employee behaviour and the increased pace of change, mean it is increasingly difficult to drive growth and create competitive advantage.

A company's intangible assets such as intellectual property, winning brands, innovative ideas and most importantly, talented staff, are now equally, if not more important than its hard assets. As Boyatzis and McKee (2005, p. 1) quite rightly noted, 'For those bold enough to lead in this age of uncertainty, the challenges are immense. Our world is a new world, and it requires a new kind of leadership'.

Information technology

Today we are faced with an overload of information, much of it digital. In a working day we may be bombarded with emails, required to be part of conference calls or called upon to use the Internet to research. Some jobs require that we use social media to advertise the company and its products. We may even be required to produce a daily blog. This is a different way of working than was the norm a generation ago.

The working lifespan has grown, with many people working well beyond pension age. This can mean that the working environment within one company has to be accessible and suitable to a more diverse workforce than ever before. Each employee will be looking to their work to provide relevant meaning for the phase of life they are currently in. Different ages and backgrounds will mean that people have experienced different cultures, styles of education and family norms and so may have come to value different things. The millennials' familiarity and comfort with digital technology and the use of a language suitable for texting and messaging may mean that short bullet points may be preferred to long reports. Younger people are more used to moving around from one job to another, whilst older people may have expected to stay in one job throughout their working life and may value more traditional and detailed reporting. Individuals' expectations of the developmental, financial and psychological rewards from their work have increased. A leader has to manage the competing demands of their workforce with its growing diversity.

Participation

People are less likely than in previous generations to accept a non-active role in the development of the company they work for. They will have an expectation (in some cases a legal right) to be consulted on decisions which may lead to changes in their conditions of service. It is now more common for there to be structures which allow consultation at all levels within an organisation. One leader may welcome such participation, whilst another may find it unhelpful, unnecessary and a threat to their authority.

Increased regulation and accountability

My father's generation recount how they designed, developed and produced goods without many of the regulations we now take for granted. We can see in the Brexit vote that many people voted Leave because of their perception of unnecessary European rules and regulations, which they considered to have been imposed on the UK by bureaucrats in Brussels. The implication in their decision is that without these restrictions Britain will be 'greater' and more productive and the belief that new or regained freedoms will bring new creativity and productivity … we shall see. Here is not the place to add to the Brexit debate or to start talking about the problems of straight or bent bananas.

However, although many regulations are questionable and potentially restrictive, the majority have been introduced to address specific needs. This is particularly true in the field of health and safety. It may be frustrating to hear that playing with conkers is now banned in schools, but due to health and safety rules we are now less likely to die as a result of a workplace accident.

Human Resources departments also have to respond to new policy demands. The number of forms that have to be completed, seemingly without any real purpose, can understandably irritate people. People react badly to being made to jump through hoops when they can see nothing on the other side of the hoop to make the action meaningful. The need for work and work processes to be meaningful is important to the whole question of creating working experiences in line with the needs of people in this century. Some of these regulations guard against people being misused by industries and organisations. We have employment rights which need regulation to back them up.

Getting the right balance, between safety and allowing for the necessary risk involved in creative and innovative development, is a key task facing a leader in this century.

Recruitment and retention

If we can succeed in finding our way through the red tape, we still have the problem of finding and keeping excellent staff. Leading into the twenty-first century, Kinsey coined the phrase 'war for talent'. Employees could no longer be seen as mere 'cogs in the wheel'. Employers had to think creatively and purposefully about how to attract and retain talented people. It is true to say that people are the most valuable resources in any organisation and their needs are becoming increasingly diverse and complex.

Indeed, businesses now have to embrace different ways of working, such as home working, virtual working, part-time working, and face the challenges of accommodating maternity, paternity, carer leave and career breaks. It is becoming more difficult to find excellent people to work in these ways, as well as in the more conventional arenas. The demand for managerial and leadership talent will undoubtedly continue to ebb and flow with the economy, but long-term trends indicate continued high growth, albeit at a slower rate. At the same time the number of available workers entering executive ranks is forecast to decline by over 14 per cent over the next ten years, as baby boomers finally reach retirement.

This has an impact on retention as well as recruitment, with Deloitte reporting that 65 per cent of executives report that they have a high or very high concern about retaining high-potential talent. To retain the most talented staff, leaders needed to have a flexible approach to achieving their organisational goals.

Globalisation

The growth of globalisation brings its own new opportunities and challenges. With our increased access to quick news people today are very aware of everything that is happening across the world. This brings fresh expectations of fairness and interpretations of trust and justice. It is now much easier to compare pricing, taxation and other processes across countries and to use this information to compete.

Trading across boundaries is nothing new. Many of us buy foreign cars and bank with overseas banks. Indeed most of Santander's customers, a Spanish bank, are from the UK. Stakeholders in companies are no longer local but global. Capital movement and accessibility is a more recent development and a major force for change. However, it does nothing to address uncertainty, as Brexit and the state of relations between global powers continue to demonstrate. We may be approaching a period of decline in global cooperation.

With Trump in the White House and other volatile leaders in power elsewhere in the world, the level of uncertainty we face is increasing.

The increased global knowledge we hold, and the potential to build global alliances has seen an increase of global activism, particularly in the areas of global poverty and environmentalism. The future is not easy to predict. Even leaders must acknowledge and work with that uncertainty. They will be required to be both creative and collaborative, both key elements in an existential approach.

Ethical concerns

Increasingly we are seeing demands for organisations to focus not just on financial success, but to take a greater responsibility for the impact of their work on people and the environment. As well as concerns about poverty and the environment, we see evidence of people changing their lifestyles in a bid to live more ethically. These changes will alter the way our industries operate.

We are already seeing this begin to happen. The growing concerns about the use of diesel and petrol fuel have resulted in the increased use of electrically powered vehicles, developments which are already impacting on the car industry. We are also seeing growing concerns about animal welfare. More people are turning to vegetarian or vegan diets, and many of those who do choose to continue to eat meat are showing increased concerns about how those animals are looked after and slaughtered. The farming industry is reacting to this by increasing free range production and introducing more humane slaughter processes. How we transport goods and the impact on the environment is now often part of the original planning process in the development of new products. What we do with products when we have finished with them is also being questioned, with real concerns about the amount of plastic finding its way into our oceans. These are just a few examples.

These new challenges require different ways of managing people and processes. Recently, people have begun to explore different approaches to leadership which are more in line with the needs and culture of the twenty-first century. These include Connective Leadership, Authentic Leadership, Responsible Leadership and Resonant Leadership. All of these draw on the identified need for greater emotional intelligence in the leadership sphere. Although each approach has its own focus, I suggest that they all share an existential approach, whether this is conscious and acknowledged, or not. I shall take a brief look at a few of them.

Emotional intelligent leaders

Most leadership models in current use owe a great deal to Daniel Goleman's (1995) work on Emotional Intelligence. In his work he gave importance not merely to the rational approach to leadership but also heralded the importance of an emotional approach which referenced intelligence, neuroscience and psychology. He called for leaders to be authentic, to have presence, to lead mindfully and to exhibit and demonstrate emotional intelligence. We see these qualities echoed in the key leadership models of the twenty-first century.

However, Goleman was not the first to consider that leadership required more than IQ and rational thinking. Aristotle identified that a great leader had the rare ability to be angry with the right person, at the right time, to the right degree, for the right purpose and in the right way. All of which call for a high level of what we may now term 'emotional intelligence'.

As early as 1920 Thorndike (1920) described 'social intelligence' as the skill of understanding and managing others. Some time later, Howard Gardner (1983) introduced the idea of multiple intelligences, in which interpersonal intelligence (the capacity to understand the intentions, motivations and desires of other people), and intrapersonal intelligence (the capacity to understand oneself, to appreciate one's feelings, fears and motivations), helped explain performance outcomes.

The first use of the term 'emotional intelligence' is often attributed to Wayne Payne's (1985) *The Study of Emotion: Developing Emotional Intelligence*. However, even before this, the term 'emotional intelligence' had appeared in Leuner (1966) and Greenspan (1989) who also put forward an EI model, followed by Salovey, Brackett and Mayer (2004), and Goleman (1995). Goleman defined EI (emotional intelligence) as a cognitive ability, that is a learned ability to perceive, understand and express our feelings accurately and to manage our emotions so that they work for us, not against us.

EI is about knowing how you and others feel, and what to do about it; to know what feels good and what feels bad, and how to move from bad to good. It requires us to possess emotional awareness and sensitivity and to develop these skills to help us stay positive and maximise our long-term happiness and well-being.

Goleman's (1995) model focuses on EI as a wide array of competencies and skills that drive leadership performance, and consists of five areas:

The first is **self-awareness** which comprises knowing one's emotions, strengths, weaknesses, drives, values and goals and recognising their impact on others, while using intuition and gut feelings to guide our decisions. This is followed by **self-regulation,** which is focused on managing and redirecting one's disruptive emotions and impulses and knowing how to adapt to changing circumstances. Next he presents **social skill**, by which we manage others' emotions in the desired direction. Fourthly, we have **empathy**, through which we recognise, understand and consider other people's feelings especially when making decisions. Finally, there is **motivation**, which allows us to motivate ourselves to achieve solely for the sake of achievement.

For Goleman, these emotional competencies are not innate talents, but rather learned capabilities that must be worked on and can be developed to achieve outstanding performance. He believes that individuals are born with a general emotional intelligence that determines their potential for learning emotional competencies.

He divided the core capabilities into **intrapersonal** and **interpersonal** aspects. The **intrapersonal** is concerned with the inner intelligence we use to know, understand and motivate others, and calls for self-awareness, emotion management and self-motivation. The **interpersonal** is concerned with the outer intelligence we use to read, sense, understand and manage our relationships with others, calling for relationship management and emotion coaching. As with existential thought they centre on relatedness and the understanding of self and others, acknowledging our freedom while calling for the recognition that any resulting decisions and actions require us to accept our responsibility for the impact of our decisions not just on ourselves but on others.

Most of the following examples of leadership flow from these principles of emotional intelligence.

Connective leaders

The oldest of these models is Connective Leadership. Lipman-Blumen (2000) believes that in order to succeed in today's changing world, leaders must adopt models of leadership which tackle the 'tensions between interdependence and diversity', as these tensions continue to escalate and impact on personal, professional, organisational and communal relationships. Previously, we were in the physical era, where physical boundaries, such as rivers and mountains, formed the barriers between groups of people. Leaders in the physical era used these barriers both offensively and defensively. Slowly there has been a shift to the geopolitical era, where geopolitical boundaries and ideologies define differences.

In the late twentieth century we saw a move into a more connective era where 'the connections among concepts, people, and the environment' (Lipman-Blumen 2000, p. 8) were tightening, and where physical and geopolitical boundaries no longer defined us or prevented us from moving from place to place, and where, at the same time, diversity, differences and interdependence were more important and vital than they were in previous eras.

Our way of living has changed, so that now, for many people, their contact with other people primarily happens at work, their ideals take shape at work and they look to find the meaning in their lives at work. At work too, life has changed and we are asked to undertake more complex tasks which demand that people use both head and heart and are competent, authentic people with meaning in their lives and a desire for high standards.

The key aspects of the Connective Leadership approach fit very neatly alongside an existential approach and share its focus on the question of meaning, the resolution of conflict and leadership development. Existential Leadership focuses on the connected themes of Freedom, Meaning, Aloneness and Death.

Connective Leadership focuses on an awareness of the historical changes in how we experience work (temporality and death). It places importance on ethical and ecological considerations (meaning, values and beliefs). As the name suggests, Connective Leadership enhances the connectivity or relatedness between different elements of business. In today's era, companies are working with collaborative and joint efforts of teams that might have members spread all over the globe. A Connective Leader has to ensure that all the different elements of the team work in a synchronised way to achieve the common goals of the organisation.

The Connective Leader needs to have a keen eye in order to identify the team members with specific skills and then assign them the jobs that can be mutually beneficial for both members and the company. It is a situation-based approach and helpful in companies that undertake projects that involve different teams that might be placed in different geographical locations. It involves forming short-term associations so the leader needs to be highly skilled and experienced in order to facilitate this practice. The model has a number of advantages. It encourages collaboration between people from diverse, even adversarial, backgrounds, helping them to work together to achieve common goals. It identifies and enables individuals with the best skill sets to be used for suitable projects and the collaborative efforts of the leaders helped to build a team whose members are able to cooperate with each other. According to this approach, everyone, the leader as well as the staff members, is fully aware of the mission and aim of the company and their role in it, thus helping everyone to stay focused and to deliver quality work. It encourages and conditions them to work in different environments with positive mind-sets, by creating an atmosphere of cooperation and reliability. It aims to give leaders opportunities to motivate the team members and remain motivated for the optimum for higher performance.

It is a flexible approach. As times change, more companies have work scenarios where teams are placed at different geographical locations and need to be managed and organised at distance according to the needs of company. A Connective Leader is equipped to handle many diverse situations and to train the team members to work in high pressure, time bound situations. The leader supports others through a high level of empathy, understanding and emotional intelligence. If we observe Connective Leaders we should see their actions as inspirational, authentic, collaborative and exploratory. They inspire others by building belief in a shared sense of purpose and vision. They are authentic, acting with honesty and integrity which builds trust. They do not hold tightly to power but seek to involve others at all levels of the process and encourage them to take responsibility. They are collaborative in that they share knowledge, seek ideas and encourage participation and collaboration and finally, they are explorers, always seeking new ideas and encouraging innovation.

However, as with all models it also has its share of disadvantages. It needs the presence of highly experienced leaders that have the exposure of working with team members or staff of diverse cultural backgrounds or skill sets. If not handled properly Connective Leadership can fail badly and create a sense of uncertainty for their future among team members, which can have a bad effect on team performance. Too much may be expected from the leader. If not handled properly the team can become totally negative and oppositional towards the leader and so not follow instructions. Constant pressures involved in connecting and exploring can make the team members feel stressed and they might start considering a change of jobs. It is an approach based on the cooperation and coordination of teams, and if that is not in place, lack of communication can happen, which can lead to a chaotic situation. When the best candidates are chosen from different teams to do a required job it can break down team identity and may not give a chance to other members of the team to be developed, or to train them for new skills.

Those leaders using a connective approach will show certain qualities and ways of being. They will:

- Encourage the development potential of others
- Deal with the ambiguities which other leaders may find threatening
- Orchestrate multiple coalitions that do not demand orthodox allegiance to their entire agenda
- Guide supporters along unfamiliar footpaths of leadership, transforming passive followers
- Offer richer vision drawn from their diverse networks
- Be personally engaged in the endless search for greater meaning
- Search for authenticity in self and others
- Be heard to ask certain types of questions which reflect their philosophical approach, e.g.

    a   What are our challenges?
    b   What are our dreams?
    c   Where is our common ground?
    d   Who will follow me?
    e   Who will support my dream?
    f   Who is different from us?
    g   Who is our enemy?
    h   What can we do for and with each other?
    i   How can we make room for everyone around the table of human reconciliation?

Connective Leadership is a style that has been successfully implemented and has generated amazing results for many of those organisations which have adopted it. However, it cannot be denied that the implementation and maintenance of this leadership style requires clarity, focus, patience and experience.

The success of Connective Leadership lies in effective communication and creating a work bond between different teams. It still has scope for improvement but overall it is a successful concept which is now increasingly chosen by more and more companies.

Authentic leaders

This approach relies on the leader building their legitimacy through honest relationships with followers whom they value highly. Authentic Leaders are not only true to themselves, but also true to their roles as leaders, which include an element of being aware of social cues and the followers' needs, expectations and desires. This is teamed with the commitment to giving and receiving and regular honest feedback (Kilduff & Tsai2003; Kernis 2003).

To be true to oneself, one has to be self-aware and continually reflect on, and challenge one's self-concept. Such critical self-reflection helps authentic leaders to know themselves and gain clarity and concordance in relation to their core values, beliefs, identity, emotions, goals and motives. These elements are not static, hence the need to continually check on them and ensure they do not become sedimented. This openness to self-criticism and commitment, to being honest, inspires trust in those looking to them for leadership.

Recently some theorists have been critical of the approach with Jeff Pfeffer (2015) of Stanford University, stating 'the last thing a leader needs to be at crucial moments is authentic.' Ibarra (2015) is also critical, believing 'We have to find a way to fake it till we become it,' and Adam Grant (2016), writes, '"Be yourself" is actually terrible advice ... Nobody wants to see your true self' (Siddiqui 2017, p. 7).

As you will have probably already gathered, I do not fully agree with these views and see these critiques as reflecting a fundamental misunderstanding of authenticity. Just as a reminder, Webster dictionary defines authenticity as 'real or genuine; not copied or false; true and accurate.' It comes from the Greek word for author, which led Bennis (2010, p. 89) to comment that, 'You are the author of your life.' I can remain equally authentic when I am dancing wildly at a party as I am when working as a consultant in traditional company. I remain the same me. We live in different dimensions, and aspects of ourselves fit authentically in all of them. Authentic Leaders are not required to tell everyone of their greatest fears or to unselectively broadcast sensitive data just because they hold it. Authentic Leaders are true in the actions they choose to take. Being authentic is not, as Grant seemed to suggest, the mindless spewing of whatever you're thinking regardless of how your words affect other people.

Being authentic as a leader is hard work. No one can be truly and consistently authentic, it is an ideal to be aimed for; everyone behaves inauthentically at times, saying and doing things they may come to regret. The key is to have the self-awareness to recognise these times and to take feedback well.

The essence of authentic leadership is emotional intelligence (EI), as articulated by Daniel Goleman. In contrast to IQ, which basically does not change in one's adult lifetime, EI can be developed. The first and most important step on this journey is gaining self-awareness. Bill George (2004) of Harvard Business School and colleagues undertook research to identify steps people would need to undertake to develop a deeper understanding of themselves in order to become authentic leaders. These include exploring their own life stories in order to understand who they are and to make meaning of their thoughts and actions. This enables the process of learning, growing, and developing an integrated self. As leaders explore their life stories and process their experiences, they develop deeper understanding of themselves and feel increasingly comfortable being authentic. In discovering their truth they gain increased confidence and resilience to face difficult situations.

George (2004) suggests that those aspiring to be authentic leaders should engage in reflection and mindful introspective practices by taking time every day to step back from the day to day world and reflect on what is most important to them. This can be done through practices such as meditation, mindfulness, prayer, long walks to clear one's mind, or simply sitting quietly and reflecting. The key is to set aside preoccupation with to do lists, electronics and the news in order to reflect privately. In this way the urgent does not take precedence over the important in one's life, and leaders examine how they are living their lives and engaging with the world around them.

One of the hardest things for leaders to do is to understand how other people see them, which is often quite different from how they want to be seen, yet, to remain authentic, leaders must seek honest feedback from colleagues, friends and subordinates about themselves and their leadership. They seek out people who will tell them the truth and offer candid critiques about their leadership. Those who surround themselves with loyal sycophants, who only tell them how well they are doing rather than being brutally honest, risk going off track.

Authentic Leaders bring people together and see their leadership purpose as aligning people around a common purpose in order to create positive impact. This is far more important than focusing entirely on achieving success through money, fame and power, yet ultimately produces sustained success in those areas as well.

They are flexible, becoming skilled at tailoring their style to their audiences, to the imperatives of the situation, and the readiness of their staff to accept different approaches, whilst maintaining their authentic values. There are times when leaders have to make difficult decisions that are sure to displease people, and they'll need to give tough feedback. At other times they need to be inspiring, good coaches, and consensus builders. These flexible styles aren't inauthentic if they come from a genuinely authentic place. As leaders gain experience and develop greater self-awareness, they become more skilful in adapting their style, without compromising their character. What is needed now is a deeper understanding of how leaders become authentic, as they navigate the practical dilemmas and paradoxes they face.

Responsible leaders

In the process of writing this book I came across the work of Tim Richardson (2015) in *The Responsible Leader* which resonated so clearly with my thinking on existential leadership. Although many of the concepts are similar the philosophical background and emphasis do differ.

As with existential leadership, Richardson is searching for an effective response to uncertainty, describing the world as VUCA – volatile, uncertain, complex and ambiguous. I certainly shall not argue with this assessment. In his response to these challenges he calls for responsible leaders to have a sense of self and clarity of identity, values and ethics. He stresses the importance of thinking and operating relationally, explaining that a responsible leader needs to be clear about his or her values and to lead with the aid of 'a moral compass'. He considers the responsible leader to be adaptable and to hold an 'orientation to learn, flex and adapt within this ambiguous world' (p. 34). As such, he calls for leaders to be 'comfortable with ambiguity and not knowing ... to be confident, open yet humble' (p. 34) and to place the attribute of curiosity, and the skill of listening, centrally within his or her skill set. You will see these key concepts echoed in my discussion of the existential approach to leadership.

He also sees responsible leadership as being 'an orientation, an attitude, a way of being' (p. 5). Existentialism too prioritises 'being', rather than simply doing. An existential leader has to embody their values in their action and live and operate authentically. Similarly, Richardson sees responsible leadership not just as a set of skills but as an approach which calls for the leader to see the bigger picture and be *intentional* (*intentionality* being a major tenet of existential thought). He is concerned with freedom and responsibility and notes that the responsible leader must *choose* to be *morally accountable*, acting for the greater good (in line with the existential emphasis on *responsibility* and *freedom of choice*, based on a set of *values*). Through this way of being the leader demonstrates care for others, thus enabling others to be creative (this links to the importance of *relatedness* in the existential approach).

Much of what I have written earlier, in relation to the qualities of connective and authentic leaders, stands true also in relation to responsible leaders.

Resonant leaders

Boyatzis and McKee (2005) consider what it is to be a Resonant Leader placing 'mindfulness, hope and compassion' high on the list of requirements. They call for a *mindful* approach that involves living in a state of full conscious, awareness of one's whole self, other people and our context. They look to the leader to maintain and communicate a position of *hope*, and to show *compassion* by understanding others' hopes and needs.

The Resonant Leader has elements of the Servant Leader, with its focus on self-sacrifice. Boyatzis and McKee acknowledge that this can often lead to burn out if the leader does not give enough attention to self-care and they term this the 'sacrifice syndrome'. They see great leaders as those who attend to their self-care needs on a number of levels – developing their intellect, taking care of their bodies and attending to deeply held beliefs and values which feed the spirit. These echo the existential dimensions I shall speak of later – social, physical, psychological and spiritual.

Boyatzis developed an Intentional Change Model which he hoped would help people to successfully engage in personal transformation with excitement and enthusiasm. It considered five key aspects:

The ideal self

- What you want out of life
- The person you want to be
- Leading to personal vision

The real self

- How you act
- How you are seen by others
- Comparison of real to ideal self
- Leading to identification of strengths and weaknesses
- Leading to personal balance sheet

Your learning agenda

- To capitalise on strengths
- Move closer to personal vision
- Work on a weakness

Experimenting with new habits

- Reinforcing and reaffirming strengths

Developing and maintaining close, personal relationships

- Develop and maintain resonant relationships.

At the core of all these approaches is the need to know oneself. That is, to know one's way of 'being' in the world, and of being with others. In the case of leaders this is particularly true. As Boyatzis and McKee (2005, p. 4) wrote:

> Great leaders are awake, aware, and attuned to themselves, and to the world around them. They commit to their beliefs, stand strong in their values, and live full passionate lives. Great leaders are emotionally

intelligent and they are mindful: they seek to live in full consciousness of self, others, nature, and society.

Although never referring directly to existential thought, this definition of a great leader contains key elements of the approach used by an existential leader. It firmly sets leadership within a relational framework (in relation to self, others, nature and society), which I shall explore in the context of four existential dimensions. It also emphasises the importance of beliefs and values, and calls for the passionate and reflective living of life. Existentialists are deeply aware of time and temporality – that we shall all die and the subsequent need to ensure that the time we have is fully, consciously and authentically lived in line with our values and beliefs.

Chapter 4

What do we mean by 'existential leader'?

Why introduce philosophy and psychology into business?

Existential leaders build their leadership approach around the existential beliefs and concerns which I have outlined earlier. This calls for a deep awareness and attention to the existential human givens – our need for self-esteem, the need to be heard, the importance of time and temporality, the core place of values and beliefs, the human requirement for meaning, our experience and dread of uncertainty, and our emotional engagement with ourselves, others and the world. If we accept that we are spending more time at work it makes sense to assume that we are tending to look for meaning, and having our existential needs met, through work more than we ever have.

Through work we may seek 'life expanding experiences' which we hope will deaden our existential fear and provide a way to transcend our own mortal death by leaving something lasting behind like a permanent footstep in the shifting sands of immortality. This is similar to the needs Covey (2004) defines as being universal for every human. He suggests every person has four innate human needs: to live, to love, to learn and to leave a legacy. Many people look to their workplace to get these needs met. An existential leader will also seek to address these needs in the way they lead.

Having briefly considered what we might understand by 'existential' and what we understand by 'leadership', you may feel that this has raised, rather than answered, a number of questions. You may be left wondering, just how do we bring those two concepts together? Where do philosophy and psychology fit in business?

On a very practical level we use psychology on a daily basis within the business world to:

- Recruit and retain the best people – choosing the right members for your team and your objectives, retaining the services of excellent staff
- Support and develop staff, consultancy, training, coaching and support
- Audit team work – to evaluate how well the team works together, to identify strengths and weaknesses of individuals and team, to work to strengths, and to identify best communication styles for greater efficiency

- Develop strategy through consultancy, assessing the human impact of change and addressing how to communicate and get buy in to the vision
- Communicate effectively using models based on understanding the communication needs and style of the person/group/organisation you are aiming to communicate with
- Prevent, manage and resolve conflict through training, coaching, mediation
- Understand power dynamics and the interplay in an individual and organisational context
- Manage stress within the organisation and the individual
- Engage in the creation of a meaningful vision through discussion and debate of shared values and goals.

The key to business development and success is understanding your main resource – your people. In order to understand them, not just as the cogs which make your business wheels function, you need to understand their psychology, their worldview. By this I mean, their values, beliefs, behaviours and preferred communication and action styles. This is not just about being an empathic person. It is not for fluffy or woolly reasons but for the benefit of the business. A business will not function successfully if it ignores psychology, but this is not enough.

Philosophy also has its place. To work existentially as a leader requires much more than adopting a set of behaviours. It is a philosophical approach, a 'way of being' which calls on the leader not just to 'behave' differently, but to 'be' different.

An existential leader has to be willing to 'go deeper' in their approach, and specifically in their relationship to others, and their search for meaning. Lipman-Blumen (2000, p. 325), in exploring what leadership is, draws attention to this, stating that 'the ongoing excavation of the leadership concept is part of a deeper search for the meaning of life, a search for how each of us mere mortals fits into the larger picture'. This need for meaning is not just a matter of concern for the leader themselves but is equally of concern to their followers. An existential leader will never forget or underestimate the importance of this.

So it would be wrong to see leadership as merely a set of strategies and behaviours which can be learnt and implemented, it is part of the serious issue of navigating human existence. We exist, and indeed, we lead within the existential constraints of finitude and our human need for meaning and relationship. Given the temporality of our stay on this planet, as a leader and more importantly as a human being, it is essential that we consider our decisions and actions carefully and take responsibility for them. Even within the knowledge of the temporality of our state the significance of the choices we make becomes greater over time, particularly where we are taking on a leadership role where our decisions can have a great impact on the lives of others.

In looking at why we have leaders at all we have seen that the terror of finitude, concluding in death itself, compels us to search for leaders to protect us, and sends us on an endless search for life's meaning. It focuses us on seeking life-expanding experiences that will, at least temporarily, obscure that fear and attempt to transcend our finite selves by leaving a permanent footprint. For many people they look to work to achieve this.

Embedded within our terror of death are the more general fears about loss of control. Our desire to transcend and control death and our knowledge that this is not possible lead us to seek control over what we believe we *can* control. Leadership offers itself as a piece in this existential puzzle. It is a symbol of security, power and control for those who lead, and for those who follow. The struggle with the power and control of leadership provides us with the temporary opportunity to turn our attention from our bodily death. Through work or other projects we can devote ourselves to something greater than self. We can imagine ourselves freed from the tyranny of egotism and need for perfection. As Lipman-Blumen (2000, p. 329) puts it, 'in the act of immersing ourselves in the greatest expression of Other, that is, some larger purpose, we emerge as our most unique selves.'

Csikszentmihalyi (1996) suggests work provides us with opportunities to act with courage, face symbolic death and experience 'flow' or 'optimal experience'. He suggests that people develop their concept of who they are, and what they want to achieve in life, according to a sequence of steps. In early life we focus on physical comfort and survival, security and self-recognition. In adolescence the focus shifts to our peers. By early adulthood we are focusing more on the relational, on our self as mate, parent, worker. Entering into midlife we become more focused on reflective individualism and from there, in later life, we face the anguish of isolation and common biological destiny which anchors us to others and marks a re-entry into the external world.

We can seek to address these 'chronological' needs through work projects in which we relate to others and to the temporality of our existence. He considered that 'Managers have turned away from traditional approaches to organizational behavior and towards existentialism, basically because they believe life is too short to fool around with. They want to be committed to something; they are seeking "engagement," or commitment' (Kelly & Kelly, 1998, p. 16).

By bringing in existential thought we create a new barter between company and employee: a new vision based on coherence and meaning; harmonious understanding of shared concerns – freedom, meaning, aloneness, death; a common reality with a concurrent vision and consideration of social, ethical, knowledge and environmental elements. Work can be experienced as a place to find meaning. We can also use it as a guard against uncertainty; through committing to a leader we can access a belief system which appears to offer a level of certainty, provide structure, offset responsibility and thus safeguard us from existential freedom by 'seemingly' limiting our choices. It may be possible to find 'life expanding experiences' in work which will deaden our existential fear and allow us to leave something permanent, transcending our mortal death.

All of these speak to the existential issues we are exploring and which have an important part within leadership. So, let's move on to explore these key elements – Relatedness, Uncertainty, Anxiety, Freedom and Responsibility, Time and Temporality, Values and Beliefs, and in the context of leadership.

Chapter 5

Leadership in the context of existential concerns

Relatedness

We experience ourselves, and everything around us, the world, other people, ourselves included, in the context of a relationship. We cannot escape others. This is true in personal and in professional life. Even if we seek solitude, this is done in relation to others. We would not need solitude if there were not other people from whom we seek space. We band together with others because we see, or seek, a commonality and a sense of belonging. We band against others because we wish to be, or to be perceived as being, different from them. Indeed, it may be that we feel that we are excluded by or from others and may attempt to regain control by excluding ourselves instead of being excluded.

In the business world these same principles apply. Even if you are the leader of your own business, working from home and not employing anyone else, you are still doing so in relation to others, be they clients or customers, competitors or suppliers. You may also need to form very positive relationships in your community for them to tolerate any noise, extra traffic and the use of parking spaces etc.

As an existential leader you must remain constantly aware of your reliance on others. Without others you have no one to lead. You are only ever a 'leader-in-relation-to-followers' just as in life you are only ever a 'being-in-the-world-with-others' (Heidegger 1962). Being and following cannot be separated, they need each other in order to coexist.

People may join certain companies because they feel that they in some way 'belong' with the other people who work there. They will assume that there are shared values and goals in play. The leader cannot afford not to understand this or to ignore it. An existential leader will seek to ensure that staff have a sense of relatedness to their colleagues and to the organisation. This relatedness will be formed through shared beliefs and values and an ethos of care for each other.

Trouble often occurs in organisations when that relatedness is threatened or seen as negative. This can happen on a personal or professional level. Just as being in relation to another may mean I have an ally, or someone with whom I can share a project and goal, it is just as easy to see others as an impediment to one's goals and therefore someone who has to be defeated. An organisation focused on competition sets its employees against one another. In the past this may have been seen as healthy competition but in twenty-first century thinking this would be considered to be a blockage to the organisation fulfilling its potential, as it is not fully harnessing the collective power of its staff. It is likely to cause conflict between individuals, often leading to stress and loss of productivity due to people taking time off sick. This can lead onto disciplinaries, grievances and employment tribunals which are costly in terms of time, goodwill and finance.

Organisations can lose valuable people when they no longer feel related. Some of my most lonely moments have been in organisational meetings. I have chosen to join organisations because they offered me a challenge whilst seeming to share my own core values and beliefs. Some of my most dizzying existential moments have been when I have been sitting with others and realised that this was not the case. This has happened when a leader is talking about a 'we' in which I do not recognise myself, or collectively speaking of values and beliefs which I do not hold.

In becoming a leader, we risk seeing ourselves as different, perhaps more successful and knowledgeable than those we lead. You may have risen through the ranks to a leadership position leaving colleagues, peers and friends behind. The role of leadership can set you apart. Leaders can take on an alien quality of 'otherness' for those who knew them in another role. This may seemingly defend leaders from distress in making some difficult leadership tasks where decisions may cause hurt or distress to some people. As leaders, it may seem easier to consider others as different from ourselves, mere pawns on the chessboard of a strategy, who can be sacrificed if needed, to win the game. Of course there is a flip side to this: existential loneliness – it is lonely at the top.

As an existential leader this presents me with the need to reflect on my relationships. I may have allowed 'non-leaders' to become 'the other', or indeed have taken on 'otherness' myself in the eyes of my old colleagues. Just like Sartre's waiter, referred to earlier (p. XXX), I may have donned the 'uniform' of a leader in order to separate myself as leader from non-leaders, so as to prove I am a leader by virtue of what I no longer am – a 'non-leader'. If I act like and look like a leader, then surely I am a leader? I shall return to this question when looking at authenticity.

In my coaching role, I have worked with a number of new leaders who found themselves in this position. Some experienced profound feelings of loneliness when they realised that people who once worked alongside them, but now worked for them, were no longer happy going to the pub with them or 'letting their hair down' in their presence. Knowing that as leader you have the power to promote or dismiss them may mean that they wish only to present themselves to you in a certain positive light. As a leader you may also feel restricted in how you feel you can behave. It is a challenge to an existential leader to address these issues in an authentic way.

An existential leader is always reflective and self-questioning. When considering the relational aspects of leadership there are a number of questions for an existential leader to ask,

- How do I address feelings of existential loneliness if I work alone?
- How do I address existential loneliness within my team?
- How am I relating to others?
- How do I relate to staff through providing support and encouragement?
- How do I maintain positive relationships when needing to constructively challenge poor behaviour or behaviour which does fit with the values of the organisation?
- Does my way of relating align with, and overtly reflect, my values?
- What am I doing to encourage and facilitate people working well together and socialising together if they wish to?
- What am I doing to encourage the development of others and myself?
- What opportunities do I facilitate for genuine sharing of ideas and concerns in a safe and encouraging environment?
- How do I understand and facilitate people's needs in relation to things and people who are important to them outside the workplace, e.g. maternity, paternity and carer leave, compassionate leave, flexi-time etc.?
- How am I encouraging appropriate team working?
- What importance do I give to the company's relationship with:
    a   its staff?
    b   its community?
    c   its environment?

There are no universal answers to these questions. They have to be governed by your values and beliefs and set within the 'thrownness' of the context in which you are leading. The organisational ethos will also govern some of your possibilities. The individual worldviews of those you are relating to also need to be factored in.

Given the importance of the relational, and the truth that my 'followers' are my most vital resource as an existential leader, I need to support them in what they do and offer encouragement, support, challenge and development opportunities. I may also feel that I need to consider their social needs. This is a difficult one.

As a coach and consultant I have worked with a number of companies who wanted their employees to 'feel part of one big family'. In one company the CEO would cook a BBQ each week for all the staff. He wanted to be 'one' to them and yet they experienced this as paternalistic and the opposite of his desire to belong, indeed they saw it as a way of showing his difference from them, as he could afford to buy all the food and be benevolent. He would also insist on the importance of attending these lunches as a form of 'team building' whilst some of the team would have preferred to have had the freedom to go home to their families or to get on with their work. It also annoyed them that in other circumstances he very clearly differentiated himself from them by either being absent, or when present by being very directive and critical.

In another company regular social events were provided for staff to interact together, with all the costs picked up by the CEO. Many of these events took place in the evening or at weekends. In both companies there were some staff members who were very enthusiastic about these opportunities, whereas others felt that they would be considered 'outsiders' or 'not team players' if they did not 'attend and enjoy' themselves. These people would attend out of fear and feel resentment about 'having' to attend and lose time they might have chosen to spend in more personal non-work pursuits. Generally they would find these social situations stressful and they would feel isolated. All of this was the opposite of what was intended. Their value systems were at odds with the CEO's, they valued family time and rest most highly and would have felt better cared for if their workloads had been more manageable, allowing them to leave work at a reasonable time.

The idea or desire to be seen as a team player is an interesting one. It is rare these days that there isn't an interview question aimed at discovering whether or not you are a good team player. As an existential leader I must ask myself what I mean when I look to my staff to be good team players. Do I want everyone to be very similar or to have the skills to relate well with diversity and to value new ideas and constructive challenge?

The fundamental question though, is how I relate to others. I need my team, and how I relate with them will dictate whether they stay in the organisation or move elsewhere. In the day to day of being an existential leader I need to check what I am actively doing to retain, develop and 'be-with' the talent in my organisation. On a daily basis, I need to question how I am supporting, developing and encouraging them. I also need to consider whether I am doing it in such a way that it not only reflects how I see things but also rather stems from an awareness of their collective and individual needs, values and sense of meaning which comes through prioritising relatedness and interpersonal communication and interest.

Uncertainty

Life is uncertain. It is uncertain in its meaning, uncertain in its future and uncertain in its essence as there exists no certainty beyond the finite nature of our existence and that all things are uncertain. Uncertainty pervades all areas of our existence. We are not able to control everything and that leaves us with uncertainty and anxiety. This may be particularly difficult for leaders, who may have become a leader in an attempt to stave off uncertainty only to find this remains an impossible task. Leaders may also be faced with the expectations of their followers that they will provide certainty, and yet the one thing we can be certain about is that we cannot truly avoid uncertainty. All this uncertainty leads to existential anxiety which we work hard to avoid.

Many of us grow up asking ourselves, what shall I be in the future? We even hear very young children, as young as two or three, being asked 'what do you want to be?' We cannot handle the uncertainty that we may not 'be'/exist in the future. We seek to plan out a future path as a way of adding some imaginary structure which seeks to offset the anxiety of uncertainty but may merely replace it with the anxiety of 'what if I can't become, or do, what I intend?' Once we have entered into a profession we may feel we have become 'something' even if what we have 'become' fails us in many existential ways.

In our personal lives we may 'become' partners or parents which can give us a sense of identity. We many have also sought some certainty through taking on these roles which bring a level of certainty. We have taken on identifiers for ourselves and others. In my psychotherapy practice I often encounter clients who are sad about their single status, or that they do not have children. Several comment that they don't want to grow old alone, or that they would like children who would look after them in their old age. One client mourned her lack of children, stating that not having them meant she was 'awash in her own life' and deprived of any of the markers or milestones which her peers who had children could look to, such as their child's first day at school or the birth of grandchildren. All of this seems to indicate a belief in a certain future, which would somehow, inevitably, unfold in a certain way if only they could find a partner, or have children. However, I also have clients who hate their partners and feel at their most alone when they are with them, others who hate their parents (one not having chosen to see or speak to her mother for over thirty years) and have no intention of looking after them in their dotage. Even when people have been lucky enough to find a person they love and have children they enjoy and get along with, there is no inevitability that this will last. I know of a number of marriages in which both the partners appeared certain of their relationship and the fact that they would grew old together, only for one partner to suddenly move out after decades of marriage. Of course we can be certain of death, and so even when people are happy and committed to stay together, it is only 'until death do us part'. The death of a beloved one throws us back into an uncertainty which we may not have been prepared for. We can be sure that there is no certainty that finding a relationship with a loving partner and producing wonderful children will address the inevitability of the existential reality of loneliness.

Many people choose to attempt to bring some certainty into their lives through their work. They have a career plan and stick to it so as to avoid any confrontation with uncertainty: 'I know my path, this is what I have to do each step of the way, if I don't deviate I shall get there'. Work becomes a shield from uncertainty but of course this is delusional. Change happens, businesses fail, redundancies happen and finally retirement happens. Along the way there will be many things which were not predicted, that are outside our control, and which shake our sense of certainty. A new leader may appear with different values and ways of being, targets may change, my role in any organisation may evolve to my liking or take me further away from what I want, new colleagues may change my feelings towards the workplace, local or global circumstances may impact on my business market. There are so many possible things it is impossible to contemplate them. So we may go with the mantra, 'best pretend things will continue as they are'!

If having a job and a permanent contract brings an illusion of certainty, how much more does this apply when gaining a leadership role? Some people choose to enter an organisation and plan to proceed up the hierarchy into leadership. Yet, they may choose never to stop and ask themselves: Do I still enjoy working here? Does the work carry the same meaning for me as it did when I entered the organisation? Am I still able to work in a manner which is aligned with my values and beliefs? Is this what I want? What do these promotions give me and what do they take away? To even contemplate these questions gives rise to uncertainty and that may feel unbearable. This may be particularly true when the entry to leadership was primarily to access greater control in an attempt to avoid the anxiety of uncertainty.

People moving into management and then leadership tend to believe that they will have more control. This may or may not be true. Yet, it is a deluded leader who believes he or she can control things and defeat uncertainty by creating organisational charts, five-year plans and complex strategic documents. All of these things may give people a false and limited sense of 'certainty'. A structure and plans are needed in business to measure development and success, but they guarantee nothing; they are mere hopes and aspirations and no matter how well thought out they are, considered against a realistic risk assessment and knowledge of the organisation and the market, they are no means 'certain'. I have written so many five-year plans knowing that the likelihood of them being fully implemented was less than 50 per cent. Having said that, there is an important place for plans and existentially informed vision statements and strategic plans, as they do provide a canvas on which the leader's values and those of the organisation can be writ large. I shall say more on this later.

An existential leader will not run from uncertainty or feel paralysed by it. They will attempt to develop an authentic relationship with it. I have spoken earlier of 'thrownness' (being placed in a context which is not necessarily of your choosing); in the work context we always have the option to leave if we don't like things but all the decisions we make carry both positive and negative implications for ourselves and for those we care about. Most of these implications can be guessed at but are essentially uncertain. When I walked away from a very well paid leadership post which no longer held meaning for me and was no longer congruent with my values, I was only too aware of the possible negative outcomes. I warned my family that we would need to cut down on everything from holidays to magazine and journal subscriptions. In the event, and I still don't know how, life continued, we still had holidays and magazines and I was a much happier person. What I had assumed would follow from my resignation was far from the truth of what did occur.

An existential leader will acknowledge the 'givens' of their position and choose to accept them or walk away. Often, this can feel like walking a tightrope on which they must lean one way and then another to retain balance and not fall. They will also need to acknowledge that they are not a god or superhero and that they cannot make an uncertain world certain, no matter how much their staff may look to them to do so. In leaving my previous post it was this sense of responsibility to my team which meant I stayed longer than I should have. I felt that by staying I could protect them from the change in values, direction and ethos of the company. They too verbalised this need for me to stay to protect them from the inevitable changes and as I result I felt I had to take on the rescuer and protector role. Of course this was as untrue as it was unhelpful to me, or ultimately to them. To ensure that we do not fall into the delusion that we hold total control and have the ability to create certainty, an existential leader should continually ask a number of questions:

- How well do I sit with uncertainty?
- How do I deal with the fact that as a leader others will look to me to address their uncertainties?
- How am I addressing uncertainty in my business? Am I using an authentic approach?
- Am I aware of the desire for certainty in those around me? Can I give authentic and appropriate answers which will reduce anxiety, without colluding with a false sense of certainty?
- Am I willing to allow my own uncertainty? Can I openly listen to criticism and commit to seeking out feedback, even if this may question my own 'certainty' about what is the right thing to do?
- How can I work positively with uncertainty, embracing its potential for creativity?

Of course it is much easier to ignore these questions and act as if the world is certain. This is not only inauthentic and delusional but also bad business practice. Uncertainty is endemic, in economic affairs no less than in other fields of human endeavour. Jefferson (1983, p. 122), when considering business decision-making wrote, 'Uncertainty intrudes heavily into decision-making which is characterised by partial knowledge; irremediable unforeknowledge; and the exercise of hunch and judgement'. This can obviously lead to dangerous behaviour by leaders often backed up by the leadership training they have undertaken. Jefferson believes that mainstream theory and business training tend to reinforce the false notion of certainty and collude in the building of a 'pretend world'. Economic theories and courses are often built on a false assumption that there is, and will continue to be, general equilibrium, perfect markets and identifiable competition. On the whole they do not take into account the uncertainty of the business future. Jefferson (1983, p. 123), speaking solely in the business context, pointed out the pressing need to 'fully accept the true nature of uncertainty and not to act in a manner which implies a greater degree of certainty and knowledge than the nature and circumstances of many business problems will admit'. To ignore uncertainty means we make business decisions built on false premises. Believing in static, linear progress has been the downfall of many businesses. We only have to look to our high streets to see the way that retailing has changed. Footfall in shopping centres is down and more goods are purchased through websites. Businesses who considered the possibility that how we shopped might radically change are more likely to have survived the change. Business needs to not shy away from uncertainty. The problem can be that many leaders dislike the very idea of uncertainty, they don't really understand what it is, and don't wish to acknowledge that profitable opportunities only exist where outcomes are genuinely uncertain. Leaders may confuse uncertainty with risk, acting as if everything was a risk and thus increasing the chance of failure. Managing risk is relatively straightforward; managing or even just accepting uncertainty is harder.

Uncertainty allows for endless possibilities and so can be seen as the midwife of creativity. Without acknowledging it, and wherever possible, embracing it, a business will slowly atrophy, working on the mistaken premise that if something is successful it is certain to remain successful if we keep doing it, and presenting it, in the same way. No company or organisation can address our existential uncertainty. We can never know what will happen today, never mind tomorrow. The company may be very successful one month and losing business the next. Yet an existential leader must work with and embrace uncertainty.

As we have noted, people working in an organisation do, rightly or wrongly, look to their work and their leaders as a safeguard against uncertainty. It gives them a meaningful project. Many welcome five-year plans and the like, to give structure, and to seemingly address fears around time and temporality. An existential leader does not need to challenge this, and force people to stand and face their existential anxieties, but also does not encourage people to look to them as leader to create a fictional world of certainty. We know and accept that plans change, but we still need them. A leader makes change a normal and vibrant part of business. Without uncertainty nothing would change and that is a death knell in business. We need to find a way to make uncertainty less scary and instead, to be approached as an opportunity for creativity.

Anxiety

I have spoken about the centrality of uncertainty in existential thought, and in the success or otherwise of leadership, and noted that uncertainty gives rise to anxiety. Kierkegaard (1981 [1844]) described anxiety as the 'dizziness of freedom'. In the business world a leader may experience a kind of nausea and dizziness when they experience their own freedom and the freedom others bestow on them by allowing them 'to lead'. This can create a false sense of certainty in leaders themselves and those working with them. Yet, as we have discovered, we are never able to truly create certainty; it is a mere illusion. A good leader has to accept that they are not all-powerful. They cannot look five years ahead and *know* where the company will be; they can only set out a vision, based on their values, beliefs and desires, and offer a path which leads in that direction. Even when they are at the 'top of the tree' they cannot be free from anxiety.

Indeed, leadership may increase our anxiety as we are taking on a higher degree of responsibility for things (the products and processes involved) and people (staff, customers, shareholders etc.). It is essential to note, identify and own our anxieties, not ignore them, and to find a way of working with them in an authentic existential way. An existential leader will not deny uncertainty or anxiety, nor will they burden others by passing that anxiety onto them. This does not mean that it is wrong to share concerns or to look for feedback and challenge from mentors and trusted individuals. Many of today's most successful leaders choose to work with external, neutral leadership coaches. The least we can do is to acknowledge our anxieties to ourselves and check whether there is any action we can take to lessen them. In many cases there may be nothing we can do but to accept the anxiety, and the uncertainty of the outcome.

In my practice as an existential therapist I have worked with many people from diverse businesses, whom others would describe as being 'the global leaders in their field'. Yet, many lived with enormous existential anxiety – an anxiety that the others who saw them as exceptionally talented were deluded and that the client may do something which exposes the fact that they are not really a good leader in their field; an anxiety that they could easily lose their leadership identity through it being taken over by another person who has achieved more than them. They may hold anxiety that they cannot truly consider themselves to be a leader until they have taken over another company, written another book, made another hit record etc. It is often difficult for these hard working and high achieving individuals to realise that, as Amit Ray (2017, p. 12) said, 'If you want to conquer the anxiety of life, live in the moment, live in the breath'. This is much harder to achieve than it sounds.

Even those individuals who are confident in themselves and their leadership will hold an anxiety as to whether this confident and seemingly secure state will continue. It may not be wrenched away from them by someone else, indeed it may be the frailty of their own human body which causes anxiety and threatens certainty through sudden illness and ultimately through death.

Having acknowledged and identified strategies to work with our own anxieties an existential leader must also hold in mind the anxieties of their followers. Leaders are engaged with their own anxiety but also, by the very nature of leadership, they are intimately involved in relationship to the anxieties of others. As we have seen, people may look to a leader to create a sense of certainty in the hope that in doing so their own anxiety will be reduced or removed. It is disempowering and counter-productive to remove all the anxieties of others, although the sense of temporarily being a superhero may feel good for a time. To try to remove all anxiety is to treat 'followers' as children and to show a lack of trust in their ability to cope. Equally, it is unhelpful to pass on every possible anxiety-making issue which the individual is unable to do anything about. As leaders, we have a duty when creating our plans to realistically consider what may go wrong and plan to counter this. We may choose to share 'givens', that is those things which may raise anxiety but can't be changed and represent the 'thrownness' of the context, for example, working to government policies or restrictive laws. One needs to acknowledge restrictions but not dwell on them. As a leader you may choose to keep them to yourself as there is nothing that someone else could do to alter them, or choose to share them with the intention being that they are acknowledged and 'bracketed' or 'put away' so that energy can be focused on what can be changed. Even an informed and reflective leader cannot predict the wide range of events which can impact on business and cause very real and practical anxieties for those working for the organisation. Knowing that one cannot authentically remove this anxiety from others may well increase the level of personal anxiety in the leader and lead to a sense of powerlessness.

The leader also has to consider their own general relationship to power, just how much they personally need to hang on to it and how much they can delegate. Some leaders feel their anxiety is lessened if they do not need to 'shoulder the whole load' and can delegate to others, whilst others feel their anxiety is increased if they hand over or share control. There are many leaders who wish to see themselves as encouraging autonomy in others but find in reality this causes acute anxiety as to whether this will result in a less than perfect outcome. If, as a leader, I hand my power over to those who follow me, I need to know how I will cope if they do not use it in a way I would have chosen, or if they make mistakes or fail to achieve the intended outcome. An existential leader will own their choice in delegating power, either appropriately or not, and will shoulder the ensuing responsibility for the outcome. They will not use the sharing of power to offset responsibility and apportion blame to others, but will stand by the actions of those to whom they delegated tasks.

Existential thought acknowledges that we live paradoxically. The delegation of power is a good example of this in the context of leadership. Having looked at the need for an existential leader to share power we also have to consider the flip side of this. A leader has to be clear about any limitations on the power and authority which they may set within the tasks delegated. Anxiety will increase if there is a lack of clarity about these limitations. In the leadership role one has to handle the reality of uncertainty and avoid false promises to mitigate the anxiety which uncertainty provokes, yet one also has to take on the responsibility which leadership brings, and not increase anxieties through lack of clarity or the changing of boundaries. One can authentically and legitimately mitigate some anxieties by being clear about expectations and through thoughtful planning. A common source of anxiety and stress is a misunderstanding of what is required and the amount of freedom given in how to achieve it, leading to the ongoing anxiety that whatever one does will be wrong.

It is not easy for a leader to know how to manage an individual's anxiety without curbing their creativity. One may have to behave differently with different individuals. Some people thrive from having clear objectives but value freedom as to how these outcomes will be achieved. Others desire very detailed ongoing instruction on what actions they should take throughout each stage of the process. As a leader you have to address to what extent you can enable these needs to be fulfilled for the good of the organisation.

Different individuals can tolerate different levels of anxiety and what causes anxiety in one person may motivate and excite someone else. Existential leaders will seek to know those with whom they work and to understand their worldview. They can enhance the possibility of the success of a project by choosing and taking responsibility for those chosen to work on that particular project, endeavouring to work with people's strengths and holding an awareness of what may raise anxiety in any individual. A leader may choose to invest time in coaching a person through their anxieties and helping them to identify strategies for dealing with them. This can be empowering for the individual and an integral part of their development programme within the organisation. Alternatively, a leader may choose to deploy someone else to the task who does not need the extra support and development. In doing so they are employing skills appropriately but not necessarily developing their team. How much time and commitment is given to this development work will be a key factor in the decision whether to go with the tried and trusted, or risk developing someone new to undertake the work.

Inevitably, there will be times when an individual will experience a level of anxiety which they may find intolerable. A leader must seek to understand the potential causes of the anxiety and consider whether these are organisational and can be addressed structurally or stem from more personal issues. My own values mean that even if the stress is not work-related I would wish to help the individual address it, perhaps by giving time off, referral to Human Resources or an Employee Assistance Programme or offering external coaching or counselling.

Often anxiety stems from a lack of the feeling of belonging. A person may feel they are no longer a 'fit' for the organisation. Business needs change, as do the needs of individuals. A business may be taken over and work to different values from when the postholder joined the company. This sense of no longer belonging or being out of synch with the majority can cause profound existential anxiety.

The meaning attached to a job may also change and the postholder may begin to feel anxiety about why they are remaining in their current post. A person may find meaning in a role purely because it allows them to meet their financial commitments. If that person then wins the lottery, they need to find a different way in which the work provides meaning. Often people are attracted to a post because it fits with their values. They may want to 'help others', 'make a difference' or 'add something creative and beautiful to the world'. They may find work places constraints on these aspirations and they are left with the anxious dilemma – do I stay somewhere which meets my need for financial security but destroys my soul, or do I risk following my dream?

Failure to understand and live with our anxiety means we focus on potential future failure or success, rather than on the truth of today. This fear can freeze us. We need to understand and heed the knowledge that 'our anxiety does not empty tomorrow of its sorrows, but only empties today of its strengths' (Spurgeon 2018, p. 186). The existential leader will be open to acknowledging their anxieties and to reflecting on a number of questions to ensure that they hold these anxieties in mind and seek to own and address them:

- How do I work with my own anxieties about uncertainty?
- What is making me anxious in my leadership role?
- Am I aware of the anxieties and desire for certainty in those around me? Am I willing to listen to them and commit to seeking out feedback, even that which may question my own 'certainty' about what is the right thing to do?
- Am I trying to rescue others from anxiety and so disempowering them? Can I risk them making their own mistakes?
- Am I expecting others to take on anxieties which I should deal with?
- If anxiety stems from lack of meaning, how am I making work meaningful for others and myself?
- If anxiety comes from a dissonance between values, am I clear about my values and those of the organisation? Do these differ from those working in the organisation and how do I address that?

As is apparent, there is the potential for the workplace to be full of anxiety. Existential awareness and the acknowledgement of the inevitability of living with uncertainty produce an anxiety that is all-pervading and never ending.

An authentic existential leader can make this manageable in the workplace without treating people as infantile. Such a leader cannot take away existential anxiety but often people find it too hard to acknowledge existential anxiety and transfer it onto multiple smaller anxieties which seem more manageable and which are within the leader's power to facilitate. This is a guard against the feeling of being out of control, which uncertainty brings, and is inauthentic.

Freedom and responsibility

We have seen that the challenge of freedom is a crucial one in existential thought. While not fully agreeing on the structure of human agency and freedom, Sartre and de Beauvoir both agreed that freedom is the core of human existence, as summarised in Sartre's statement that 'existence precedes essence'. If it is so central to how we see our existence it is equally important in how we see and exercise it in a leadership role. We need to consider how we can lead authentically and thoughtfully within both the core existential issues of freedom and responsibility.

We have earlier considered leadership as a perceived potential shield from the existential anxiety caused by freedom. If others are to look to you to protect them from anxiety it may be quite attractive to don your superhero cape and act as though this were a real possibility. So, we must start by truthfully considering our own stance in relation to freedom, the limitations on that freedom and the responsibility which accompanies it. We need to also consider the extent of the freedom we may wish to give to others. Their autonomous action will have an impact on how we feel about ourselves, how we perceive others and the success of our overall leadership.

Some leaders are happy, even eager, to share freedom and power with their 'followers', whilst others fight to retain overall control. Both stances may be welcomed by different people, or at different times. Some leaders and some followers will love the challenge of shared responsibility. This may come from the leader's core values including a desire to empower others or from a wish never to carry sole responsibility, being fearful of getting it wrong and being blamed for their decisions. Others may be reluctant or even determined never to share freedom and responsibility. A leader may feel that their leadership conveys the right to make autonomous decisions which others are required to implement. They may experience suggestions for doing things differently as a challenge or even a sign of disrespect for their authority. Followers may feel that a leader is paid to lead and should get on with that task instead of shifting or sharing responsibility. These different stances can put pressure on any leader.

Followers often perceive the leader to have a great deal more freedom than they have. Many like to believe that the leader has 'total' freedom. If this were the case then we could just transfer total responsibility to the leader in the way an infant may need to do to an adult. In reality parents know that they do not hold the ultimate power which their children invest in them, just ask any parent who is trying to potty train their infant! A parent cannot stop their child from becoming ill or feeling pain either physical or psychological. They can do things for their children but in doing so may limit their freedom. Children are prevented from putting their hands in the fire but need to be given the freedom to take some risks or they fail to grow into independent adults. One of the tasks of parenthood is knowing how much freedom to give, and at what time. This is equally true in the leadership role.

In my own experience of leadership there have been times when I have felt my freedom limited more than it was when I was not in a leadership role. For example, in theory in one position I 'controlled' a very large budget but that responsibility was always a shared and limited one, although it may not have appeared that way to others. I knew how I would have liked to allocate the money but the reality was that I needed any proposals to slowly wend their way through a number of committees before being signed off. I had to lead within the limitations (thrownness) of government policies and organisational rules and regulations. Even so, I retained the freedom to disobey the rules and risk the consequences, or ultimately to hand in my notice.

A dilemma of leadership is the extent to which one is authentic and truthful about the limitations of your power and freedom. In my leadership roles I have chosen to share what I termed 'givens' which were the limitations on freedom which I chose to accept in order to release funding or allow developments. These contrasted with the other freedoms I had which were not subject to such restraints and for which I held sole responsibility or could choose to share with others.

Freedom can present a harsh challenge to leaders. I have always strongly held the value that we should give excellent service to our clients. However, in my early years as a leader this did tend to mean that at times I limited the freedom I gave to some of those working for me. I would rewrite reports which I did not consider to be 'good enough' and so as not to offend the authors would not mention that I had done so. Eventually a valued colleague challenged me on this, pointing out, quite rightly, that by doing so I was not allowing people the freedom to make their own mistakes. I was in fact disempowering them. This critique was hard to hear, as also central to my values was the desire to empower people. My own self-esteem was the reason I was not willing to let reports which were essentially 'good enough' pass through to committee level. I was afraid that it would reflect badly on my leadership and management. Yet in attempting to avoid this I was not authentically working within my own values and was limiting others' freedom to develop. I took a deep breath and gave others more freedom. I let reports which were acceptable, but not inspiring, pass through and discovered that there were no repercussions and that several of the authors gained courage and continued to improve.

Most people value a level of autonomy within clear boundaries. As an existential leader I must be clear as to where an individual's freedom is limited, why and in what way. It is better to draw the limits from the beginning rather than let someone run with an idea only to be told later that they had no authority to do so. People also need the safety of knowing whether or not they are free to take creative risks. They need to know that you, as an existential leader, will back them if these risks fail. Therefore, an important question for any existential leader to answer is: does your leadership inspire freedom and courage, or create fear? As an existential leader I need to continually check whether the freedom I give is positive. Am I encouraging creativity through delegating or am I in fact merely getting rid of work I do not fancy doing myself? I need to create and maintain trust so that my team can expect that when given freedom they will also receive encouragement, support and helpful feedback, not destructive criticism.

In giving freedom it is inevitable that at times, people will not do things exactly how you would do them. You need to examine how you will feel and deal with this. For some non-existential leaders they would prefer people to fail rather than do something better than how they would do it. The success that others gain through using their own initiative and doing things differently may be experienced as a threat to the leader's self-worth, authority, power and importance. Everyone has a need for self-esteem and if a leader is to give others freedom to succeed then they must be willing and able to welcome their success not just for the person who has created it, but also for the leader who was not afraid to facilitate it.

New times need new approaches. The way we define work is changing. This calls on leaders to consider what freedoms they will allow in how people work. More leaders are allowing employees autonomy as they integrate their home and work lives through a number of measures including the ability to keep non-traditional hours, work from home, take sabbaticals or unlimited vacations. Technological changes have changed the way we work. We can communicate with one another through email, text, Skype, conference calls and the like which do not require us to be in the same room at the same time. Being open to hiring telecommuting employees can open up a talent pool previously limited by geography as well as reduce costs associated with having employees on site. These new ways of working require the leader to give employees greater autonomy and to trust that they are equally invested in obtaining a successful outcome. Learning to trust that an employee seeks meaning in his work and wishes to do it well can be a challenge. It takes the willingness to let go of some control, and perhaps even change the criteria used to determine if the work is getting done successfully. The question is no longer whether a leader can see an employee sitting at a desk for eight hours, or spot his car in the car park, but whether the employee is producing the work they're supposed to, on time, and to expectation.

Leaders may not always find it easy to sacrifice control. In business, freedom can be seen as a blessing and/or a curse. If we encourage, or merely allow, employees to have a degree of freedom we can encourage creativity and a sense of responsibility and ownership. For some leaders this is a very frightening prospect. Also, for some employees this is a challenge too far and may feel unfair, as they may believe that the leader is paid to carry that level of responsibility. It can be difficult to define exactly what freedom means and yet it can be equally challenging, and perhaps paradoxical, to define its boundaries.

Freedom in the workplace can encompass the continuum from creating the vision together, through to implementing it by exercising creativity, to suggestions as to how to approach immediate job goals, and even the encouragement to constructively criticise management, leadership and the status quo. Giving employees a role in developing the organisational vision, and allowing them the room to identify and reach their objectives in the ways they see fit can be a solid leadership move if done right. Designing channels for freedom of speech, including constructive criticism and making suggestions for change, may challenge the leader's vision but can result in considerable benefits and business innovations.

There are several reasons why some companies are embracing employee autonomy. Charlie Harary, partner at venture capital firm H3 and Company and a business professor at the Syms School of Business at Yeshiva University, saw companies taking cues from successful companies like Google, whose reputation for innovation has been linked with less conventional work environments. He spoke of the ever growing 'millennial workforce' with their different take on work and very high expectations for learning, development, transparency and flexibility. He believed that to get the most from this group and increase their work satisfaction it was important for leaders to respond by giving them freedom to manage much of their own work and to determine when and where they do that work (Harary & Dagostino 2018).

When leaders talk about freedom their hope is that the commercial outcomes it produces will be positive for the business as well as the individual. Leaders need to be clear about what they want and why. Mark Thompson, an executive coach, suggested that innovation, reciprocity and loyalty were the key business needs, all of which call for a level of freedom. Innovation requires the freedom to be creative, to experiment and to risk making mistakes. With reciprocity there has to be a belief that leaders and followers are equally committed to a common cause and that it is possible for both to make some of their own choices and own the outcome. Loyalty flows from a shared belief in the values of the organisation, and the experience of being valued and 'invested in' by the company. Thompson (in an unpublished speech in 2006) pointed out that 'if you want people to stay after all the training you've invested in them, then you've got to reward them with some freedom', and he suggested that the resulting high performance could be achieved through consideration of '3Ps' – purpose, passion and performance.

From what we have learnt so far about existential core issues, you will see how well these suggestions line up with the existential focus on meaning (purpose and passion) and freedom. Purpose and passion are to my mind interlinked. A team needs a purpose. It needs to be clear why it is engaged in the process it is and what leaders and customers want from the company's products or services. As Thompson put it, the team needs to 'use your freedom to understand how your customers want freedom too'. This of course links with what has already been said about the need for clarity in relation to reducing anxiety. When thinking of passion, this directly relates to the existential emphasis on the meaning employees give to their work. Thompson believed that if a leader does not know where that meaning lies then 'the freedom you give is pointless'. Considering performance, we have already seen that creativity needs freedom to blossom and bring innovation to business performance.

The degree of freedom given is often a cause of disagreement. In my work as a mediator, the issue of freedom has been present in many of the disputes I have worked with. This is often between a manager and a person working directly to them. Conflict has often arisen because the employee feels unfairly constrained, disrespected and not trusted. From the manager's perspective they feel their authority is under threat if they allow a level of freedom to the person working to them. This is often the case with newly promoted managers, where they want to flex their new authority, and will be inclined to *tell* someone to do something 'because I say so and I'm the boss'. If we remember the importance of meaning then we can clearly see why this does not work. Understanding the reason why you are being asked to do something and why it has to be done in a certain way can be seen as an existential need required for a task to be meaningful. If it is not meaningful, yet doing it a different way would provide meaning, an existential leader would want to facilitate the freedom for it to be done in a new way and would value the learning which came from that.

These concerns in handling freedom give rise to a number of questions for leaders:

- How important to me is the freedom my leadership gives me to act freely and autonomously?
- How willing am I to share that freedom?
- What do I fear in giving freedom?
- What do I see as the risks and gains in giving freedom to others?
- How do I deal with my ego, if having been given freedom, people do things better than I would have done?
- Can I hand over control to others when appropriate?
- What will I do if I don't like what they do with that power?
- How do I respond when someone challenges my ideas or me and plans?
- How do I handle my own need for self-esteem?

- How do I encourage people to take risks?
- What do I do to encourage creative dialogue?
- How do people know they are welcome to make suggestions for changes or for new business ventures?

All freedom carries responsibilities. Leaders hold responsibilities to themselves, their followers and those important to them and to the environment. An existential leader is faced with a number of questions around the boundaries of their responsibility:

- Where do I set the limits on my responsibility?
- Does it stop with my responsibility to the organisation?
- Do I owe a responsibility to staff?
- Does this include their physical and mental health?
- Does it include a financial responsibility beyond their work hours?
- Does it include their training and development?
- Do I hold a responsibility for the quality and nature of the services or goods we offer?
- Do I hold responsibility for the environmental impact of the creation, use and disposal of our products and services?
- Do I hold responsibility for the environment of my organisation, including the physical workplace and the land around the workplace?

A leader carries the responsibility to lead and to accept the consequences. This is also true when the leader has delegated actions to others. A leader will share failure and success whilst carrying the ultimate responsibility for the outcome. Giving freedom and responsibility to others may require the leader to encourage, or even push, people out of their comfort zone, increasing their trust in themselves via the trust a leader is placing in them. It is reported that Theodore Roosevelt, when considering what made the best executive, suggested that it was a person with the sense to pick good men to do what he wants done whilst having the self-restraint to keep from interfering with them while they do it.

Time and temporality

Our awareness of time and temporality reminds us that we are only temporarily on this planet and that we move through phases in our lives. We are not here for long, things existed before us and things will exist after we are gone. Experiencing the temporality of life evokes what Heidegger calls anxiety. As we have seen, this ontological anxiety is hard to tolerate and we can try hard to evade it through abdicating truth and responsibility. This is as true in the work context as it is in the rest of our life. Many people look for meaning in work because we are not immortal and we seek ways of making our temporal stay on this planet meaningful. As most of us have financial commitments and psychological needs we choose to work. We may spend more of our waking hours at work than we do with our families.

Our fear of death is present in lots of 'mini deaths' which we must encounter along the way. It could be the death of a relationship; the death of a career through redundancy, retirement or being discharged; death of a hope or vision; death of an ideal, death of status etc. Throughout life we will suffer many of these endings, some we will have chosen, while others will be forced on us. Having a job and being occupied can save us from a constant awareness of the temporality of our lives. We measure our time by the hour we arrive or depart from the office, the amount of time allocated to complete a task or attend a meeting. If I am focused on these small time frames I can avoid looking at the most terrifying one: the space between my birth and my death. I may become preoccupied by the milestones and timed assessments I may be measured by. These may be irritating but they do move my focus from my existential anxieties and perhaps offer false certainty that I know what I will be doing tomorrow when of course I do not even know that there is a tomorrow.

Being an existential leader requires one to remain alert to time and temporality and its potential for causing anxiety. Nothing lasts forever and our role as an existential leader in a particular context will inevitably come to an end. Many people feel that a leadership role enables them to create or access an easily understood self-identity, which will be maintained. When asked *what* they are, they can reply, 'I am a leader in x organisation' and to the question 'what do you do?', they can reply 'I lead'. Even if this told us anything about *who* a person is, it is merely a temporary identifier. When I decided to make a career move from a post where I was clearly a designated 'leader' to another where I would be working alone, I was surprised by the number of people who asked me how I would cope with the loss of identity and the lack of structured time. I had never really considered that, for some people, my job gave me my identity or that people might feel that I looked to my job to negotiate the daily passage of time. I was always more interested in 'being' than 'doing' and never engaged well with the question 'what do you do?' Having said that, those who worked with me would consider that I was always busy 'doing' as well as 'being' and would probably have liked a little less of the 'doing' from me! I am also acutely aware that 'doing' is in itself a defense against temporality. However, I consider that I am so much more than my job title. What I do under the title of 'leader' is only one area in which I express who I am, not the entirety of my being. Who I am remains the same as time shifts but the context and manner in which I express myself and am encountered by others changes.

All this is important in the context of considering time and temporality and how we 'are' as leaders. Many people spend a lot of time and energy becoming a leader, but do not think about what that means and what psychological impact it may have firstly when they gain that title and then when they no longer have it.

Some time ago I suffered a wake-up call from this drifting through time. Carl, a senior colleague of mine, died suddenly at the age of 42. He was a well-liked, healthy man who worked hard and treated people fairly. After a day at the office he had returned home, told his wife his leg was aching and retired to bed to 'put his feet up'. A short time later his wife found him dead after suffering a thrombosis.

I had always enjoyed meetings in Carl's room. He had brought in a beautiful large, wooden table from home. He kept the table beautifully polished and laid out on it were several separate neat piles of work papers. Each pile had a gorgeous stone holding the papers in place. Each stone was smooth and had fault lines of wonderful pastel shades. Carl had collected these on his holidays and brought his favourites into his office. For months after he died the door to his office remained open and the piles of papers and his precious stones remained untouched. He was not replaced. His work was distributed amongst those of us left in the team. No one spoke of his death (or his life). Each time I passed that office door and saw the stones I was reminded that we all die and that things continue without us. Carl had been an excellent employee but once he was gone, he was gone.

This brought about a radical rethink for me and I asked myself a number of questions: What was I working for? Did I still enjoy it? Was it meaningful? What did I want people to think or say about me when I was gone? What were my priorities? Over a period of time I decided to train as a psychotherapist and to leave the work I had been doing for many years. I was asked by many people how I would deal with the loss of a high, reliable salary, a guaranteed pension and what they saw as a high status and high profile job. They asked whether the *timing* was right as they believed I had achieved a lot so far, and to 'give it up' was to *lose time*, to go back to the beginning and spend many years retraining. Carl's death had made me realise that none of these things really mattered to me. Carl had not lived long enough to enjoy that pension. His status and salary had not prevented his death. My work was no longer enjoyable or meaningful and I did not know how long I had left. It was *time* for a change. I asked myself what kind of legacy I wanted to leave, what would I like to have in my obituary? I was certain that if I had died that day I would not have liked the obituary I would have left behind. I thought about what I would like to be said about me and set about changing my working life to give more of a chance of leaving a legacy that would be meaningful to me.

Fortunately, we may not all encounter the finality of the death of an individual in our work but we cannot escape 'mini deaths' which will evoke grief and a sense of loss. When funding for a project is withdrawn, or a project is successfully completed, we have come to the end of something. When we encounter redundancy or retirement we are experiencing significant endings.

All change requires endings and beginnings. An existential leader will be aware and sensitive to this and the consequences for those involved.

A leader has to work with the knowledge of their own temporality but an existential leader will also consider how time and temporality sits with those they are leading. We have seen that many look to leaders for security, which in some ways is a denial of time. No one can guarantee anything about the future, yet the leadership role requires us to act as though this were not the case. How we manage others' needs for certainty and time lines, set within a belief of continuity, may present a problem to an existential leader. Yet, in life we need meaningful projects and paradoxically we need to proceed with a sense of a future, no matter how vulnerable that may seem, and with the certainty that things end. It is the same in business; as leaders we are usually required to have five-year plans and strategies, we have goals attached to timed outcomes, we have to determine budget allocations without truly knowing how circumstances and priorities may change over time. This can feel uncomfortable and inauthentic to a leader trying to work existentially, yet it may be the only way of progressing things in an organisation which thinks linearly. There may be a tension between authenticity with regard to time, and one's values and passion to undertake the work one believes in.

I always found the need to overtly own and share these tensions and paradoxes with my teams. I could not guarantee that my plans would unfold over time exactly in the way I had described in my various strategic plans (in fact all I could guarantee was that they would not!) but I could honestly state that the plans were my intention. As with life we have to live each day as though it were our last but also prepare for that not being the case. This was a lesson shown to us by early AIDS patients who were virtually given a death sentence. Some lived life to the full as though there was no tomorrow, spending what they had, but then found it hard to adjust and find meaning when new medical advances gave them the possibility of a 'normal' life span.

Time and temporality create a number of questions for an existential leader:

- What is my own relationship to time? Is it a constant threat to my projects?
- How do I address temporality and time to create a structure on which uncertainty can safely sit?
- The role as leader is only temporary, if I invest too much of my sense of self and meaning in my leadership role, how will I find identity and meaning once that role ceases?
- What responsibility do I have to consider the meaning of time for an individual I need to make redundant or a colleague who is retiring?
- How do I prepare myself for the time when I shall no longer in work?

Time has a business meaning, and a metaphysical meaning, and an existential leader will hold both in mind.

Authenticity

As we noted earlier, existential philosophy, as shown in the works of existential thinkers and writers such as Kierkegaard, Heidegger, Nietzsche and Sartre, places considerable importance on holding true to oneself and one's beliefs and values despite external pressures. More recently, Kernis (2003) identified four components of authenticity – awareness, unbiased processing, action and relational. 'Awareness' is in relation to our motives, feelings, desires and self-relevant cognitions and includes being aware of (though not limited by) our strengths and weaknesses, traits and emotions. By 'un-biased processing', Kernis means not denying, distorting or ignoring internal experiences and external information. Our 'action' and behaviour must be authentic and in tune with our true self, our beliefs and values. Lastly, as with the rest of our existence, authenticity is relational. Our authenticity as a leader will be shown in our engagement with ourselves, others, the world and beyond.

An authentic approach relies on leaders building their legitimacy through honest relationships with followers whom they value highly. Authentic leaders are not only true to themselves, but also true to their roles as leaders, which includes an element of being aware of social cues and followers' needs, expectations, desires and feedback (Kilduff and Tsai 2003; Kernis 2003). Having such a trusting relationship can at times feel uncomfortable. Leaders have to make difficult decisions that are sure to displease people. Authentic leaders have to give regular and truthful feedback, which at times may be quite challenging and tough. At other times they need to be inspiring, good coaches and consensus builders. These flexible styles aren't inauthentic if they come from a genuinely authentic place.

In addition to holding an awareness of others, to be true to oneself, one has to be self-aware and continually reflect on, and challenge one's self-concept. Such critical self-reflection helps authentic leaders to know themselves and gain clarity and concordance in relation to their core values, beliefs, identity, emotions, goals and motives. These elements are not static, hence the need to continually check on them and ensure they do not become sedimented. Openness to self-criticism, and commitment to being honest, inspire trust in those looking to them for leadership.

We have all encountered times in life when we feel the pressure to appear to be a certain kind of person, adopt a particular mode of living or ignore one's own moral and aesthetic objections in order to have a more comfortable existence, 'to fit in'. This can be particularly true in the workplace and at times when we are representing others, including the organisation for which we work. On occasion I have described leadership as a feeling of walking a tightrope of authenticity and truth. To walk a rope successfully one cannot be static and stand upright, one has to flex and move like bamboo along with the rope. But even bamboo will break. A leader has to choose how far they can bend their values for the good of self and others before the feeling of inauthenticity is too strong and they must step down off the rope before they fall.

As leaders, people will have expectations of us and how we will behave. We may be instructed that there are certain things we cannot mention; we may be expected to deny business rumours which we know to be true. We need to own our decisions and may choose to stay in work situations that don't match our values and where we feel uncomfortable because we can't give up the security the job offers us. These decisions to stay are not in essence bad, but to be authentic they must be recognised for what they are, and the decision to stay must be acknowledged as a choice.

Both Kierkegaard and Nietzsche noted the human need to find something to believe in. For some this comes from a work goal but existentially the individual must stand alone and take responsibility for actively shaping their own beliefs and making a decision on how to proceed if these are in conflict with organisational values. Transcending the limits of conventional morality and attempting to live as a free thinker and speaker can be a challenge in the workplace. We are increasingly seeing brave examples of 'whistle blowing' where people are risking job security to be authentic and to act in line with their own values, but more often than not they suffer in a material way as a result. To say nothing would no doubt bring a different suffering as a result of living with inauthenticity.

We can note and acknowledge these paradoxical challenges. Alternatively, we may choose to ignore them and live in what existentialists may term 'bad faith'. We need to examine and take authentic responsibility for our decisions. As Socrates pointed out 'the unexamined life is not worth living'; it wouldn't be possible to live an *authentic* unexamined life. Erickson (1995) and Heidegger claim that it is not possible to be fully authentic and instead speak of the 'level' of authenticity in a person. No one can be truly and consistently authentic; it is an ideal to be aimed for. Everyone behaves inauthentically at times, saying and doing things they may come to regret. The key is to have the self-awareness to recognise these times and to take feedback well.

An existential leader will seek to find ways to appropriately and authentically give people the freedom to safely be true to themselves, to mould direction, to take responsibility for actions and to speak out against things they do not agree with. Once again this isn't easy, as authenticity calls on us to share leadership power whilst taking full responsibility and it challenges any illusion we may hold that we are *totally* defined by circumstances, culture, gender, family, organisational policies etc. Their authentic actions strongly influence individuals' ability through motivation and stimulation towards better performance and, as a result, individuals perform at the peak of their strength and efforts.

Experiencing authenticity in a leader fosters the development of authenticity in followers, contributing to their well-being and the attainment of sustainable, true and authentic performance (Gardner et al. 2005). Authentic leaders lead from a framework of moral values and ethics and a high regard for those they work with. When they make mistakes they own them to avoid these mistakes in the future (George 2004).

Leaders who remain authentic demonstrate Positive Organisational Behavior (POB) through concentrating on people's strengths rather than weaknesses (Gardner & Schermerhorn 2004) and providing a role model for the company's values which should be mirrored in organisational structures and behaviours. Gardner et al. (2005) quoted Warren Buffett, the chairman of Berkshire Hathaway, who sent a memo to his CEOs in which he indicated that 'they could lose money, even lots of it but they cannot afford to lose reputation for honest and high ethical behaviour, not a shred of it!' He went on to say that it took Berkshire Hathaway 37 years to reach a third place ranking in terms of the most admired companies in the world, and that 'an *inauthentic* action on the part of the leaders at Berkshire could result in a catastrophic loss of reputation in less than 37 mins!' (Ovide 2011).

Although, as we have seen, Pfeffer did not see authenticity as useful to leaders in crisis, Ibarra advised leaders to fake it, and Grant, warned leaders that no one was interested in seeing their true selves, as you will have probably already gathered, I do not take this view and see these critiques as reflecting a fundamental misunderstanding of authenticity. It is not necessarily about telling everyone everything all of the time or blurting out one's emotional insecurities; it is about honesty and acceptance that a leader is not a superhero who can defend against uncertainty and death.

Existential leaders will regularly interrogate themselves as to their level of authenticity and ask themselves a number of questions:

- How do I remain authentic with others when I move up into a leadership role?
- Am I hiding behind the uniform of my leadership rather than relating authentically with others?
- Am I making myself too busy to reflect on how authentic I am being, by preoccupying myself with to do lists, electronics etc.?
- Do I surround myself with people I know will agree with me, or with people who will challenge inauthentic behaviour?
- What am I doing to seek honest feedback from colleagues, friends and subordinates about my leadership and myself?
- Do I make time to engage in reflective and mindful introspective practices by stepping back and reflecting on what is most authentically important to me?
- What criteria do I use to judge my own authentic practice?
- What are my truthful motivations in any of my leadership actions, e.g. if I delegate, is it to develop others, use resources appropriately, or to guard against taking responsibility?

Leaders' styles and behaviours are the outward manifestation of their authenticity. As leaders gain experience and develop greater self-awareness, they develop flexibility, becoming skilled at authentically tailoring their style to their audiences, to the imperatives of the situation, and the readiness of their staff to accept different approaches. George (2004) suggests that what is needed now is a deeper understanding of how leaders become authentic, as they navigate the psychological challenges, the practical dilemmas and paradoxes they face. The psychiatrist David Cooper (2007, p. 96) stated, 'perhaps the most central characteristic of authentic leadership is the relinquishing of the impulse to dominate others'. It calls for a truthful alignment between what you think, say and do as a leader.

Values and beliefs

In the previous section I focused on authenticity. This raises the question as to what I am being authentic in relation to. I would suggest that the baseline for checking my authenticity is my values and beliefs. It is my values and beliefs which give my life, and my leadership its meaning.

In the 1990s organisational theorists such as Edgar Schein and Karl Weick were exploring the centrality of 'sense-making' or as I might term it 'the search for meaning' in organisations and their cultures.

Schein (1992), taking an anthropological view, focused on the corporate culture of the organisation, which he experienced as an all-embracing phenomenon at least partly determined through the leadership and in turn the culture then going on to determine the style of leadership. Such an approach is concerned with the metaphors, myths and stories which become embedded in the organisation and which reflect its meaning. Indeed, Schein identifies the leader as 'a manager of meaning'.

Weick (1995) introduced 'sense-making' as a key issue in the field of work and organisations, arguing in line with existential thought that people are constantly trying to make sense of the contexts in which they find themselves. He identified seven components in 'sense-making'. He saw it as grounded in the construction of identity and concerned with a person's sense of who they are in a particular context (or existential dimension). It is essentially retrospective, in that the perceived world is a past world in which things are visualised before they are conceptualised; that sense-makers create their own environments for future action; it is grounded in the relational, and set in a social context in which people are influenced by the presence of others; it is ongoing, people are thrown into the middle of things and forced to act; it is resourceful with people elaborating cues into stories that selectively support initial views and, finally, that it is driven by plausibility rather than accuracy, being concerned with coherence and how things hang together with certainty that is sufficient for present purposes.

Thomas Mengel (2012), in looking to develop leadership models combining emotional intelligence and existential analysis, also placed the need for meaning at the heart of his thinking. He directly linked this to values and beliefs. He considered the work on motivational psychology, an area not normally immediately associated with existential analysis. He uses the Sources of Meaning Profile (SOMP; Reker, 1996) and the Reiss Motivational Profile (RMP; Reiss 2000) as means of allowing individuals to identify and prioritise areas of meaningful engagement and actualisation based on values to build a leadership development model based on Existential Motivational Analysis (EMotiAn). Reiss (2000) identified a set of 16 basic desires and values that motivate and underlie our actions:

- Acceptance, the need for approval
- Curiosity, the need to think
- Eating, the need for food
- Family, the need to raise children
- Honour, the need to be loyal to the traditional values of one's clan/ethnic group
- Idealism, the need for social justice
- Independence, the need for individuality
- Order, the need for organised, stable, predictable environments
- Physical activity, the need for exercise
- Power, the need for influence of will
- Romance, the need for sex
- Saving, the need to collect
- Social contact, the need for friends (peer relationships)
- Status, the need for social standing/importance
- Tranquillity, the need to be safe
- Vengeance, the need to strike back.

These link well with existential concerns, as I have aimed to show in Figure 5.1.

Just as in existential thought, Reiss saw the understanding of a person's values as being essential in understanding that person and thus in leading them. He holds the strong belief that to motivate another person, you have to identify, understand and appeal to their values. This may seem obvious but it is not universally practised. Reiss gives the example of a football coach who tells his team that their next game will be a test of character. In his research Reiss found that in reality this team did not care much about their character. So the coach was vainly trying to appeal to values which were not held by the group he was trying to motivate.

Agapitou and Bourantas (2017, p. 26) suggest that 'existentially intelligent people will be more motivated due to their higher sense of purpose', and that motivation will be initiated in response to existential angst. They link existential angst to the Ancient Greek concept of Eros: 'the capacity to follow what is most intensely missing or unfinished in our lives', that which contains most value for us. This is associated with intrinsic motivation and the human capacity for learning and creativity.

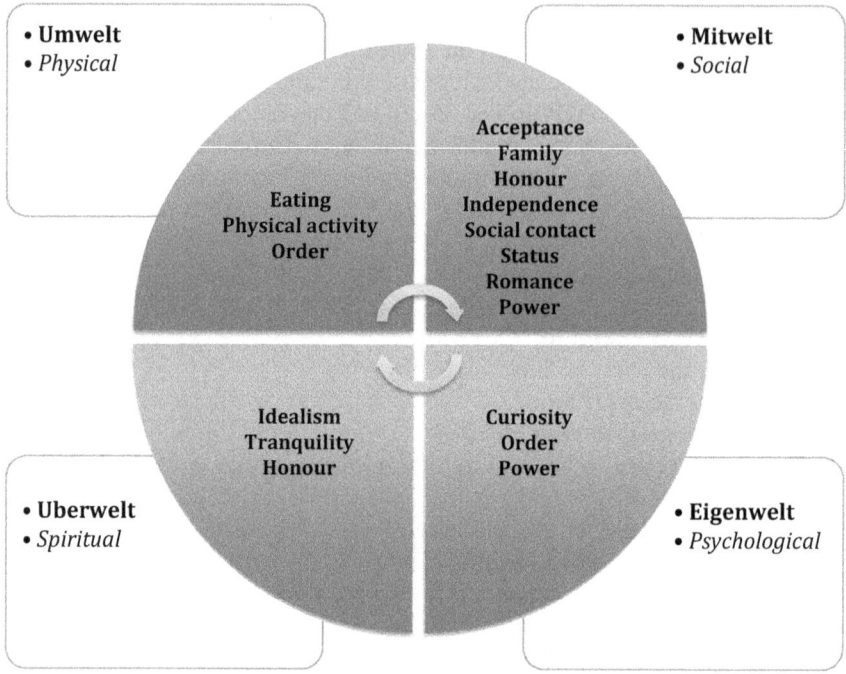

Figure 5.1 Overlap of existential dimensions and Reiss motivating values
Hanaway and Reed (2014)

Our values are so important to us as individuals that we tend to believe that they are best, not just for us, but for everyone. If we find something works for us, or excites us, we tend to believe the same will be true for others. Although we all share a set of existential givens (i.e. death, temporality, anxiety, need to be heard, search for meaning, isolation), we need to remember the existential belief in the uniqueness of each individual. When I learn something about myself, I would be wrong to assume that I had learnt something which is a given in human nature. What I have learnt is something which sits well with me as an individual and with my values. As a dog lover, I may assume that if someone's dog has died they will be sad, when in fact they may be relieved and may never have liked their dog. In business the desire to win provides an excellent example – although competitive people like to win, many others dislike judging or being judged and are de-motivated by competition as it is opposed to their values.

Sedimented beliefs, action patterns and values

Our values are important and will influence our behaviour and leadership style but, if not regularly examined they can become stuck or 'sedimented'.

'We can be dogmatic or stuck to such an extent that it is often hard to realize that there might be other ways of viewing the world or other ways of conducting our lives' (Strasser and Strasser 1997, p. 91). When we speak of things being sedimented we mean they have become stuck, only capable of being shifted with some effort. Our beliefs and values, plus the behaviours which stem from them, can become sedimented. Behaviours always stem from, and thus reflect, our values. We behave in a certain way because we feel it is a good thing to do, morally, economically or for some other value-led reason. We may unquestioningly hold onto values and behaviours which have served us well in the past and fail to recognise that they are no longer working for us. It is hard to accept that tried and tested ways do not always work and that some values are questionable in the behaviours they may lead to. We may hold a value of 'loyalty', believing it important to be loyal to a person, a concept or an organisation. If I have a total belief in the value of loyalty, what happens when the person I am being loyal to behaves in a questionable way? Where do I stand if an organisation I am loyal to uses its earnings to fund something I think is dangerous, or it doesn't treat its employees well, breaks health and safety or employment legislation etc.? Do I remain loyal to the person/organisation or loyal to my belief? This is a situation which has confronted many 'whistle-blowers' and one I have personally faced.

Another personal example of needing to explore my own sedimented values was presented several years ago, when I led a very large department. I tried to lead in a transformative and collaborative way, aimed at developing and empowering those working to me. I chose to provide a framework for a vision which would be built collaboratively with my leadership team and then aimed to inspire the wider team through our enthusiasm. I met briefly with each of my senior managers once a week to discuss how they wanted to achieve the elements of the vision which they led. I did not mind how or where they did things, if it was at home with a glass of wine that was ok, as long as the outcome was high quality, on time and fitted with the values embodied in the vision. I disliked being directive as I considered it to be disrespectful and patronising to senior managers and could indicate a lack of trust in their abilities.

A new senior manager, Jim, joined my leadership team. He was a very structured individual. He would arrive at 8.30am sharp and leave on the dot at 5.30pm every day, regardless of where he had got to in his tasks. He rarely moved from his desk throughout the day. After a few weeks I was concerned that none of his work objectives were progressing. Each week I asked how things were going and I would usually be told 'fine'. I might provide suggestions about how things may be progressed, but another week would go by without any development. After about six weeks I told Jim I was concerned at the lack of progress and his general lack of engagement in what we were working towards. He responded that he had done 'everything I had asked of him'. I was shocked and responded that for me it looked as though he was ignoring everything we had discussed. He repeated that he had done everything *asked* of him. This time I got his point. I had in fact not *asked* him to do anything. I had suggested, encouraged and discussed but never *asked*. I checked that I understood correctly that he would only do things he was *asked* or specifically *told* to do. He confirmed that was the case and that as leader he expected me to instruct and order him to do things.

This presented me with a dilemma. I held two equally strong values which in this instance were in competition. I believed in respecting others, and until now that had meant not telling them what to do. I was proud that my team always delivered high quality work and met any deadline. This was important because the work we did had a direct impact on disadvantaged people and if we didn't deliver, then people suffered. With Jim it seemed that I was going to have to put one value above another. If I was to give a good service to the client I had to be directive with Jim, telling him exactly what to do. My short-term decision was to alter my management style with Jim to a more authoritative transactional model in order to fit with my value in relation to the client.

In order not to feel that I was acting in bad faith I needed to be authentic with Jim. I explained to Jim that working that way was not something I was comfortable with. It was against my personal and professional values. However, I was willing to work in a directive way with him as it was important to me that our clients did not suffer and he had told me that in order for that to happen he needed me to behave differently. I checked that he understood that it meant I would be treating him differently from the rest of the senior managers because he has specifically requested that. We agreed that we would go ahead using this different approach.

I was also interested to know his feelings about the organisation's vision and strategy as he had arrived after they had been agreed and he had therefore not been part of their creation. Yet again Jim provided me with another challenge. He told me that he really 'didn't care about the vision, he would implement any vision he was told to implement'. Given the nature of our work, and my own values and preferences, I had dangerously assumed that people joined this particular organisation because they had a passionate belief in the work we did. Jim told me he 'would be just as happy implementing a strategy for Tesco as he would for a global charity'.

Looking at Jim in relation to management theory, he was not relationship-focused (McGregor Y theory) in his work style, as were the majority of my team. He leant more to the task-focused (X theory) although the completion of tasks was clearly not a high priority; he wanted structures, timelines and details before he could start anything. Jim put me in the position where I could not allow my values to be sedimented and so had to rethink and prioritise them. By serving one value 'respecting autonomy and creativity in my team' I would sacrifice another 'providing a high quality service to the clients'. I had to choose to stir up at least one value! In the event, using a different management style with Jim did not bring about any real positive change and he chose to leave the organisation shortly afterwards. Despite this,

I did not regret my decision. My values had called for me to respond to, and try to understand, the worldview of another person and to work in a way which allowed their way of being to be respected. At least with Jim I knew I had tried.

In a more overriding business context, it is essential to challenge sedimented beliefs and values to ensure that the company does not get stuck in the status quo. To be dynamic in business we must constantly be questioning and open to change: Are my beliefs correct? Is the company based on values which are still meaningful? The failure to reflect and question puts the business at risk.

The first opportunity to overtly demonstrate your values as a leader will be in your organisational vision statement. Every leader is called on to formulate, communicate and then lead the implementation of a vision which others can follow. This may be a political vision, a religious vision or a commercial/media vision (a vision which allows for the development of a commercial market stemming from music, film or other media). The very first steps in creating this vision will demonstrate your values. Is it a vision which has miraculously come to you and in which you believe wholeheartedly and do not wish to change in any way? Or is it a vision which you want to co-create with others?

When a business draws up its vision it needs to take into account the universal need for meaning which we have been considering. A vision statement is a company's declaration of meaning. It is a road map which indicates where the company wants to go, what it wants to become, and how it wishes to be seen. It is inspired by its values and beliefs and provides a guiding direction for the company's growth. I devote a chapter in my forthcoming book *An Existential Approach to Leadership Challenges* to the development of an existentially based vision statement.

Some value-led questions which an existential leader may wish to reflect on might include:

- Are my personal values in opposition to any of the organisational values?
- How do I respond when one of my values is in tension with another?
- How do I regularly check that my values have not become sedimented?
- How do I ensure that I lead an organisation based on values and thus providing meaning for everyone within it?
- Do I know the values of my team members?
- How often do I challenge my own beliefs?
- Are my values clear to those who work with me, to our clients and to our community?
- Does my vision statement reflect my values and beliefs?
- Is the way I relate to people in line with my values and beliefs?
- Do I know my breaking point? How far can I flex my values and beliefs for the good of the organisation or those working in it before being inauthentic?

Meaning

As we have seen in the previous section in relation to the work of Mengel, our values and beliefs are the foundations from which we build meaning. Mengel (2012) looked to develop leadership models combining emotional intelligence and existential analysis. In doing so, he looked to Frankl (2003) for inspiration particularly, *Man's Search for Meaning*, which Lipman-Blumen also alludes to. He drew attention to the need to give more recognition to this search when considering leadership, positing that the human 'Will to Meaning', the centerpiece of Frankl's (2003) motivational theory, and its application within Frankl's Existential Analysis, can serve as one significant aspect of leadership. This places the emphasis on the role of leader as motivator and as a person who offers a potential level of meaning. He draws specifically on Frankl's three dimensions:

- Creating something meaningful
- Experiencing something as meaningful
- Reframing something as meaningful.

Frankl believed that we discover meaning by answering the questions 'why?' and 'what for?' The answers are based on our personality and on the situational context we find ourselves in. This shows the importance of values in leadership processes, and the need to create meaningful work environments (Mengel 2008). Frankl's work was also the basis for Reker's (1996) 'Sources of Meaning Profile (SOMP)' through which individuals can identify and prioritise what is meaningful to them and how their values can be actualised.

Working from this, Mengel also looked to the work of Steven Reiss in the field of motivational psychology. Reiss (2000) discovered that the pleasure principle does not suffice to describe human behaviour. He reviewed philosophical and psychological traditions from Plato to Maslow, including Frankl, and suggested that pleasure and happiness are by-products of experiencing life in general, and our behaviour in particular, as meaningful. He created the Reiss Motivational Profile (RMP) in which he identified a set of 16 basic desires and values that motivate and underlie our actions, believing that this, together with Maslow and Frankl's work, might form the basis of a model of Existential and Motivational Analysis (EMotiAn).

While there is no agreement on one particular definition of leadership, many approaches see leadership as being a process of influencing oneself (self-leadership) or others to actualise particular values and/or to demonstrate certain behaviours. Therefore leadership can be described as being comprised of the abilities to analyse and evaluate a given situation and context, and make decisions accordingly through understanding different behaviours, needs, achievements, beliefs and values, and through this to facilitate the integration of personal, organisational, and other contextual values in a way that is *meaningful* to all involved. This requires us to be relational with regard to others and self.

This has consequences for the development of leaders aiming to analyse, evaluate and use a person's existential sources of meaning and their profile of basic desires in the context of their current situation. Any tensions and potentials need to be identified and addressed to enable a better match of existential values and basic desires and the contextual situation. It falls within the work of the leader to enable a better existential understanding of an individual's needs and the identification of a professional pathway to increase meaningfulness. More recent writing on leadership points to a growing acknowledgement that organisational performance and successful leadership are dependent not so much on finding the best idea, structure or model but more on the energy taken in discovering what matters to people. Porras, Emery and Thompson (2007) discovered when they interviewed a number of successful leaders that most saw the role of leadership to be about making a difference, creating something which lasts and being engaged in meaningful and fulfilling activity. They argue with the dictionary definitions of success, definitions which they consider are 'a potentially toxic prescription for your life and work' which make no reference to meaning and happiness nor to 'feeling alive while engaged and connected with a calling that matters to you. No thoughts about a legacy of service to the world' (p. 19). These were all aspects of leadership vital to their interviewees and that we would expect to find in an existential leader.

For the existential leader the making of meaning and enabling others to find meaning in the workplace is essential. Indeed, John Seely Brown, no academic philosopher, but the Head of Research at Xerox Park for over twenty years, defined leadership today as being 'not just to make money, it's to make meaning' (Gill 2010, p. 147). When we find something meaningful we are invigorated, we 'get into the zone' or experience a 'flow experience' in which everything fits. If we can find what makes us tick, what gives us meaning, and integrate it into our leadership role we become passionate about our leadership. We can then look to ways to extend that sense of meaning throughout our organisation, starting with our vision and mission statement through to our recruitment and development of staff and the environmental context in which we work.

Existential leaders will reflect on certain questions:

- What meaning does my work give me?
- How do I make work meaningful for those I work with?
- Do my statements, policies and actions have a desire for meaning at their heart?

- How will I transfer the meaning I place in my leadership role to something else when I am no longer a leader? Am I preparing for this change?
- How do I address people's needs to move on if they seek meaning elsewhere?

Some leaders will not see any of these considerations to be within their leadership role and yet they make for a more productive organisation and form a core part in the thought and behaviour of the existential leader.

Chapter 6

Existential leadership skills

It may well seem strange setting the word 'skills' in an existential context, as generally they appear to be more about 'doing' than 'being', yet we cannot exist or develop without acquiring skills. As a toddler we learn the important skills of walking and talking. We learn social skills, how to get along with others, which behaviours are tolerable in which circumstance. These skills extend the parameters of our being and our relationship with others. They may be intuitive but benefit from encouragement and practice. So, when I write of 'skills' I do not mean the acquisition of formulaic systems of behaviours aimed at achieving an outcome. I am focusing on important, yet simple 'skills' which an existential leader 'embodies' rather than 'uses'. They are authentic and stem from the leader's values.

All the skills I am focusing on are relational. They are about the leader's interaction with other people. Some companies focus on 'products' and 'processes' but somewhere along the production line from innovation to production of those commodities people are involved. This is true even in the most automated of industries. At the very least there is a person involved in deciding what the product is and committing to buying the machines necessary to make it.

We have already noted the increased focus on the skills in emotional intelligence when recruiting to leadership roles. Before I turn to explore how an existential leader may work with emotions, I want to spend a little time looking at what might be termed Existential Intelligence. Gardner (1999, p. 271) described existential intelligence as 'having a heightened capacity to appreciate and attend to the cosmological enigmas that define the human condition, an exceptional awareness of the metaphysical, ontological and epistemological mysteries that have been a perennial concern for people of all cultures.' Gardner, a developmental psychologist and a professor in the Harvard Graduate School of Education, developed a theory of multiple intelligences, offering a definition of intelligence as 'the ability to solve problems, or to create products, that are valued within one or more cultural settings' (Gardner 1983, p. x). In his original work, undertaken in relation to teaching and education, Gardner identified seven distinct intelligences, two of which were later additions. The theory emerged from cognitive research and documented the extent to which students possess different kinds of minds and therefore learn, remember, perform, and understand in different ways. He defined the nine intelligences as:

1. Naturalist Intelligence (Nature Smart) – The human ability to discriminate among living things (plants, animals) and show sensitivity to other features of the natural world (clouds, rock configurations).
2. Musical Intelligence (Musical Smart) – The capacity to discern pitch, rhythm, timbre, and tone, enabling us to recognise, create, reproduce, and reflect on music. There is often an affective connection between music and the emotions.
3. Logical-Mathematical Intelligence (Number/Reasoning Smart) – The ability to calculate, quantify, consider propositions and hypotheses, and carry out complete mathematical operations. It enables us to perceive relationships and connections and to use abstract, symbolic thought; sequential reasoning skills and inductive and deductive thinking patterns.
4. Existential Intelligence – The sensitivity and capacity to tackle deep questions about human existence, such as the meaning of life, why do we die, and how did we get here.
5. Interpersonal Intelligence (People Smart) – The ability to understand and interact effectively with others, using effective verbal and nonverbal communication, the ability to note distinctions among others, sensitivity to the moods and temperaments of others, and the ability to entertain multiple perspectives.
6. Bodily-Kinesthetic Intelligence (Body Smart) – The capacity to manipulate objects and use a variety of physical skills. This involves a sense of timing and the perfection of skills through mind–body union.
7. Linguistic Intelligence (Word Smart) – The ability to think in words using language to express and appreciate complex meanings. It allows us to understand the order and meaning of words and to apply meta-linguistic skills to reflect on our use of language. It is the most widely shared human competence.
8. Intra-personal Intelligence (Self Smart) – The capacity to understand oneself and one's thoughts and feelings using such knowledge in planning and directing one's life. It calls for not only an appreciation of the self but also of the human condition.
9. Spatial Intelligence (Picture Smart) – The ability to think in three dimensions using mental imagery, spatial reasoning, image manipulation, graphic and artistic skills, and an active imagination.

Where individuals differ is in the strength of these intelligences – the so-called profile of intelligences – and in the ways in which such intelligences are invoked and combined to carry out different tasks, solve diverse problems, and progress in various domains. Gardner (1983, p. 17) defines existential intelligence as 'a concern with ultimate life issues ... the capacity to locate oneself with respect to the furthest reaches of the cosmos'. Using it requires engaging with the existential features of the human condition ... the significance of life, the meaning of death, the ultimate fate of the physical and the psychological worlds, and such profound experiences as love of another person or total immersion in a work of art. Initially Gardner was a little unsure about including the existential realm in his nine intelligences. It was not one of the original seven intelligences that Gardner (1983) listed in his seminal book, *Frames of Mind: The Theory of Multiple Intelligences*. However, after an additional two decades of research, Gardner (1999) decided to include existential intelligence in his book, *Intelligence Reframed*.

Existential intelligence, also referred to as 'spiritual intelligence' or 'cosmic smarts', relates to an individual's ability to use collective values and respond intuitively to and understand others and the world around them. To use existential intelligence requires a willingness to tackle those challenging existential questions such as the meaning of life, why are we born, why do we die, what is consciousness, or how did we get here?

Agapitou and Bourantas (2017, p. 19) suggest that existential intelligence is characterised by certain properties which most people equate to leadership characteristics – scope, clarity, strength and consistency. By 'scope' they mean the 'range of big questions for which the individual generates and develops assumptions/beliefs and values'. 'Clarity' refers to how clear and solid the answers to these basic questions are. 'Strength' lies in the conviction held in relation to the answers they formulate. 'Consistency' is 'the harmony between values and beliefs ... so that an articulated and comprehensive image about self and cosmos is obtained'.

I do not agree that the formulation of assumptions and holding to those consistently are necessarily existential. An existentialist will continually question assumptions and therefore may also change them. The consistency is more likely to be around values and beliefs, but even these will be questionable as they can pose paradoxical questions – for example, if I believe in loyalty, will I follow a leader even if I do not agree with their actions?

People who excel in existential intelligence are able to see the big picture. Philosophers, theologians, *leaders* and coaches are among those that Gardner sees as having high existential intelligence. They demonstrate a number of characteristics such as questioning the nature of everything; using self-talk while working; being calm and showing a tendency to prioritise values and spiritual (not necessarily religious) beliefs.

Both emotional and existential intelligence may be considered as being to some extent innate, but both are capable of being developed if we wish to, and give the time to it. As existential leaders we must ponder the more difficult aspects of life and ask ourselves difficult questions, discussing everything which occurs around us related to humanity, fairness and spirituality/meaning and seeing its place and relevance in the workplace. Indeed, it could be said that no intelligence is more significant in the workplace than the existential. It is concerned with leadership issues – the intelligence of the big picture, of contexts and connections, and goes beyond mere cognition, to human intuition and archetypal themes that provide each of us with meaning, dignity, integrity and aspiration. It is concerned with giving work meaning and purpose through authentic action and development.

We live in a society which is constantly shifting. At the time of writing, when the UK has voted for Brexit (something it does not understand, and it seems no one can define) and we have President Trump in the US, it may appear to many of us that the focus on learning, development, relatedness and authenticity is no longer valued. The 'threat' of uncertainty is being countered by thoughtless defensive reactions. However, no civilisation continues to develop without all of Gardner's intelligences. There is a natural correlation between the skills valued in the twenty-first century workplace and the paths to human learning and productivity. They call on Gardner's multiple intelligences and are relational, emotional and at heart existential.

Existential intelligence creates the baseline for the other existential leadership skills and I am going to start with a skill you already have, but which you may not be fully using to facilitate your leadership.

Using listening

So far, I have focused on a number of existential aspects which are important in leadership. Perhaps one of the key ones is 'relatedness', which includes how we understand, communicate and work with others. It is likely that in whatever leadership role we find ourselves we are reliant on others to work collaboratively with us to fulfil organisational goals vital to our leadership position. How we recruit, retain and enable the development of these collaborators is vital to the success of the organisation. To relate, we need to be present to others and whatever leadership style is in use. There is one skill which is fundamental to successful leadership – communication.

Studies tell us 70 per cent of mistakes in the workplace are a direct result of poor communication. It has certainly been my experience as a mediator that lack of communication, poor communication or miscommunication lie at the heart of the majority of disputes. So, the key to good leadership is communication, and the key to communication lies in listening. It is the doorway into another person's world. If you value someone, then you listen to them. What better way to show people that you value them and the contribution they make than to *show* them that you are listening? Kerpen (2017) considers that if you want to succeed in business and in life, you need to focus less on yourself and more on other people, that is, be interest*ed* instead of interest*ing*. He calls on leaders to listen actively instead of thinking about what you want to say next. By letting people know that you have heard them you validate other people's thoughts and emotions, and their right to express. This does not necessarily mean agreeing with them. When employees say they want their voices to be heard, they are really saying they want leaders who will not just 'hear', but really openly 'listen' to them. I don't know how many of you have suffered, as I have, those consultation meetings when a company is going to restructure. Government and company policies, and union arrangements *require* consultation, particularly where redundancies might be a result of change, so organisations are getting very good at holding consultation meetings where they dutifully hear what people have to say, whilst not listening, as the decisions have already been made. For those trying to honestly express their views and concerns this charade is worse than not holding a consultation at all. It is disrespectful and arrogant and yet it is far from unusual.

It is not just in these more procedural times that employees need to be listened to. Businesses benefit from regular, on-going open and authentic listening embedded in workplace practice. Today, employees seek more attention, feedback and support and leaders need to embrace this as it builds a collaborative approach, rather than an 'us and them' split. Leaders who listen create trustworthy relationships that are transparent and breed loyalty and provide a safe space for creativity.

So, if I found myself in a position to appoint the perfect leader, who would inspire trust and encourage creativity and innovation, I would prioritise the necessary leadership skill of listening. As a leader I need to listen to the experience of others, be they other leaders, or followers. I listen to increase my understanding and to build rapport. If people feel understood they feel valued, if they feel valued they will in turn value, respect and, if it is meaningful to do so, will follow. Most people respect leaders who listen because they know how difficult listening can be. We can see the importance of effective listening when we consider a few statistics:

- 85 per cent of what we know we have learned through listening
- Humans generally listen at only a 25 per cent comprehension rate
- In a typical business day, we spend 45 per cent of our time listening, 30 per cent of our time talking, 16 per cent reading and 9 per cent writing
- Less than 2 per cent of all professionals have had formal education in learning to understand and improve listening skills and techniques.

Unfortunately, listening is a leadership skill that seldom appears in leadership job descriptions. Those who do listen to their employees are in a much better position to lead the increasingly diverse and multigenerational workforce. The 'one-approach-fits-all' way of thinking is outdated and those who embrace the art of listening are likely to be the better, more compassionate leaders and pick up some ideas useful to the business along the way.

Currently, if a company wants to know the skills and attributes of a potential worker they call in external specialist recruitment agencies, or increasingly, organisations use psychometrics to help them in the recruitment of staff to managerial and leadership positions. Psychometrics is a set of tests which aim to show the characteristics and skills of individuals and are often used to group people into 'types'. One of the most commonly used, and one you are likely to be familiar with is 'Myers-Briggs'. This is based on Carl Jung's (2017) archetypal psychological types. Myers-Briggs groups people around the ideas of introvert and extrovert personalities, although Jung warned us that, 'There is no such person as a pure introvert or extrovert. Such a person would be in the lunatic asylum' (Richard 1982, p. 192). However, Myers-Briggs starts from the premise that we have a leaning to introversion or extraversion. There is a lot of information out there about the Myers-Briggs preferences and related psychometric tests, so I am not going to go into these here.

Those of us drawn to existential and phenomenological approaches tend to resist any labelling and may be quite skeptical of many psychometric tests. We seek to understand another person not through tests but through being present to them in order to understand and respond empathically and authentically to their uniqueness. We aim to use listening skills to explore their worldview, which we have learnt is focused on their values and beliefs which in turn inform their behaviours, coping strategies, communication and action styles.

If I can fully listen to an applicant at interview then I don't just hear about their transactional skills, but I can also pick up on the extent to which their values match those of the organisation. I can gain an understanding of ways in which a job might be meaningful to them, therefore increasing the likelihood of making a good appointment of someone who is likely to feel a sense of belonging and so stay within the organisation for some time.

Once we have recruited someone, it is very common to see leaders who believe they are in dialogue but are dominating conversations rather than listening. They may believe that because they are in the position of power they should do most of the talking. They may be skilled at talking *to* not talking *with*. When someone tries to make a point such leaders often either cut them short or override them, simply because their position means they can and they fear that their self-esteem may feel damaged if they hear something new or something which questions their existing beliefs and assumptions.

Often leaders see meetings as an opportunity to inform everybody about their brilliant new ideas. They don't give people the chance to give their views and offer their ideas and so eventually people stop trying to express them. So many good ideas and innovations are lost because of leaders failing to provide people with the space to talk and failing to listen if they do. An existential leader values the uniqueness of the individual and will facilitate the expression of unique and innovative ideas, seeing them as a major asset in the development of the organisation. It is a terrible waste of an organisation's most valuable asset – its staff, not to do so; after all, they are the professionals with experience at the coalface. Not listening to their opinions is hindering, as opposed to promoting, progress. Worse still, it will de-motivate them and make them feel as if they are not worth listening to. Not giving your full attention to an employee when they are talking is the equivalent of saying 'you are valueless and unimportant'. This will eventually create a negative workplace where people feel unhappy and disaffected, creativity will be blocked and as a result productivity will suffer.

The fear of listening and not knowing what might be heard is a defense against uncertainty. In my work training mediators I come across many lawyers wanting to retrain. They have been taught never to ask a question they don't already know the answer to – in effect, not to listen at all in case they hear something which makes them question their assumptions and so makes life more difficult. As leaders we may feel that we know what we know and we don't want that challenged. Any challenge may be experienced as a threat to authority. Often leaders who do not listen are demonstrating a lack of confidence, a desire to talk so much that there is no space for someone to question what is being said. It is only insecure leaders who are afraid to listen. They demonstrate insecurity and inauthenticity in relation to their own ideas. If they really were so certain of their rightness there would be no threat in someone offering a different perspective.

There is little doubt that good listening, where you need to put your own material to one side and focus on what the speaker has to bring, is good business. It motivates your staff and encourages them to share their experiences and ideas with you. It energises them by showing they are valued and can leave them eager to do a good job. Leaders must also listen to their clients, not just trying to 'sell' what the leader has to offer, but also seeing what it is the client really needs. Failing to listen can waste a lot of energy on producing something no one wants.

We show we listen in very basic but essential ways. We have probably all had that experience where we have been speaking to someone and they are going through the pantomime of nodding their heads while they look over their shoulder to see who they ought to go to speak to next. We may also have experienced the listener who is full of positive encouragement, 'that's brilliant ... really interesting' etc., yet you know if you asked them what you have just said they would not have a clue.

So, what is good active listening? Ralph Nichols (1980) of the National Listening Association stated, 'the most basic of human needs is the need to understand and be understood. The best way to understand people is to listen to them.' So listening is about seeking understanding, not about gathering facts. An important part of listening is to be authentically interested in what the other person is saying and to have the ability to communicate to that person that you are genuinely interested in and really do want to understand their particular point of view. We already use these skills every day, without thinking. If you ask a small child what we listen with they will tend to point to their ears. This of course is a good starting place, but we also 'listen' with our eyes and our nervous system through which we feel. Many of these skills are very subtle and happen through eye contact, facial expression, nodding, posture, tuning in embodied feeling and not interrupting. We need to let the person we are listening to know that we value their expression through showing presence – good eye contact, consciousness of our body language and through checking out that we really have heard them, rather than assuming we have. We can do this by paraphrasing or summarising what we have heard so that we provide an opportunity for correction or expansion.

Unfortunately most of the time we are in too great a hurry to understand, and without checking back we tend to believe we understand too quickly, responding with one of the most irritating comments, 'I understand'. We cannot fully understand another person because everything they say is infused with their values, beliefs and past experiences. If I am going to say this, I should always clarify what my understanding is – 'I understand that you think/feel ... because ...'. This allows the other person to correct any misunderstanding or to build on an understanding which is incomplete. If I don't clarify the level of my understanding I am relying on an understanding that is informed by my own values and life experience rather than an understanding that is based on the other's values and point of view. To listen well we must *be empathic, engage, be open minded, mindful and respectful.*

When you care about your employees, they tend to work harder and aim to exceed your expectations. Employees want to be led by those who genuinely care about who they are and what they represent to the team and organisation at large. They are not merely tools and resources for your own success but individuals who bring unique capabilities and aptitudes not necessarily limited to their job functions. It is a human need to be heard and when this is missing our stress increases. In the workplace this can lead to depression and sick leave with all the negative impact this brings to a business. Empathy is a powerful display of listening. Many leaders avoid emotional interactions, but the best leaders know how to empathise and make themselves approachable to those who need attention.

Putting time and energy into listening makes leadership easier. The reputation of a business depends upon listening skills. If you fail to listen to a customer, it can tarnish the company's reputation and lose business. Listening can reduce conflict which can arise when an individual feels misunderstood or mistreated. Early listening can stop conflict escalating. Listening helps to improve morale and productivity by understanding what motivates each employee and what they find meaningful. Through an active listening approach based on these ideas we can achieve a number of objectives helpful to the leadership process. We can:

- Create rapport and trust
- Show that we are really trying to understand
- Demonstrate respect and interest
- Reveal what really matters to the speaker
- Enable the speaker to hear him or herself.

Having seen that active listening can be of benefit to the organisation, how do we do it? Firstly we must address anything which may get in the way of our listening:

- Being tense, nervous, anxious or feeling insecure
- Trying to remember everything that is being said!
- Worrying about our 'performance'
- Working out what to say next or what to do
- Wanting to rush to a conclusion
- Bombarding someone with fact finding questions
- Assuming we understand too quickly, from our own point of view.

If distracted from listening, an existential leader will seek to become aware of what is causing the distraction. They can then try to 'bracket' what is getting in the way. The term 'bracket' in this context comes from Husserl (German: *Einklammerung*; also called 'epoché', or phenomenological reduction) and is a term in the philosophical movement of phenomenology describing the act of suspending judgment about the natural world to instead focus on analysis of experience. Epoché (εποχή, epokhe, 'suspension') is an ancient Greek term which, in its philosophical usage, describes the state where all judgments about non-evident matters are suspended in order to induce a state of ataraxia (freedom from worry and anxiety). Visually it may help, once you spot yourself feeling bored or impatient, or feeling the need to rush the person or make a judgement, to simply visualise putting them in brackets as in a sentence (…). Once we have challenged ourselves to exercise bracketing we can start to attend to the speaker and tune in to what they are saying, thus learning more about their worldview.

Fortunately, it is an existential given that all human beings wish to express themselves and be heard. I have already spoken about the existentialists' interest in the phenomenological approach. Phenomenologists, drawing on the work of Edmund Husserl (1859–1938), based their understanding about how they and others exist in the world on the premise that we interpret something so that it can be identified and have meaning and that the objects exist through the meaning that we give them. This is known as 'intentionality', which occurs unconsciously. Husserl (2009) saw every act of intentionality as containing two parts: the noema and the noesis. Noema is directional, the object (the what) that we direct our attention towards and focus upon. Noesis is referential, the *how* through which we define the object. Perhaps an easier way of thinking about it is to say that the noema is focused on the perceived facts of the experience and the noesis on the felt/emotional way in which the individual experiences the event and gives the content unique meaning. If we understand that both these aspects are present then we see that when we are listening we need to listen for and to both aspects – the facts, and the way those facts are emotionally experienced. We also need to note that both these aspects are going to be interpreted by the individual through the veils of their familial, cultural and individual experiences and through their value sets and emotional context. Many leaders fail to show any interest in the noetic, whereas existential leaders will make this their primary focus in learning more about an individual and in building trust.

As existential leaders, what are we listening for?

One of the many things, indeed maybe the main thing, you are listening for is the expression of emotions. We are all emotional. Emotions are always present but there is often a desire to conceal them. Some people are more comfortable expressing emotion than others. Emotions play such a big role in our lives that there are more than 600 words in English to describe them verbally, not to mention 43 facial muscles to express them physically. If we gain insight into a person's emotional world we discover how central and important an individual's value system is.

Emotions are always attached to something, whether the object is within the person's consciousness or not. The object or person they are attached to is usually linked in some way to values and beliefs. We often feel at our most emotional and at our most vulnerable if our beliefs or values are attacked in some way. The attack may come from others, or from ourselves, when we find ourselves behaving in ways which go against our beliefs. By understanding this about ourselves and others, we can identify emotional stressors and may need to acknowledge the tensions inherent in holding values and living and working in a particular context where these may be strengthened or attacked.

Academic research involving major companies and government leaders points out that emotions do not just 'appear'. The research suggests that many of the ones that arise in your everyday communications stem from five predictable core concerns: appreciation (recognition of value), affiliation (emotional connection to others), autonomy (freedom to feel, think, or decide), status (standing compared with others), and role (job label and related activities). I am sure you can hear the echoes of the existential concerns alluded to earlier. By addressing those concerns proactively, you can steer a potentially negative conversation to a positive place and thus extract greater cooperation from your superiors, colleagues, and those reporting to you.

If we gain insight into a person's emotional world we discover how central and important an individual's value system is. Emotions are always attached to something, whether the object is within the person's consciousness or not. The object or person they are attached to is usually linked in some way to values and beliefs. We often feel at our most emotional and at our most vulnerable if our beliefs or values are attacked in some way. The attack may come from others, or from ourselves, when we find ourselves behaving in ways which go against our beliefs. By understanding this about ourselves and others, we can identify emotional stressors and may need to acknowledge the tensions inherent in holding values and living and working in a particular context where these may be strengthened or attacked.

We are not seeking to challenge the values expressed, but to use the knowledge to understand how these values and beliefs are being played out within the current situation and the future organisational plans. To enable someone to fulfil their potential, having gained trust and rapport a leader must challenge any ambiguities or rigidity and work towards future action which takes account of the values of the individual.

Another important aspect of human behaviour, which we need to understand and listen out for, is the way in which an individual copes with challenging situations. Most people have a set of identifiable behaviours which they use in their approach to life. These may include; competing, accommodating, avoiding, collaborating and compromising (Deutsch 2000). They are usually most transparent in people's public worlds and the world of work and can be seen in the stances taken to teamwork and to management and leadership. In the world of management theory they are labelled as transformational (which is facilitative and would include accommodating and collaborating) and transactional (which is directive and more geared to competing).

One can begin to see how important it is for an existential leader to understand and take a transformative stance. Most leaders would seek to develop a team who are flexible and creative. This may require them to move from one behaviour pattern or coping strategy quickly when faced with different individuals and different problems.

Whatever their designated role within an organisation, people often choose to adopt a coping position as a 'leader' or a 'follower'. For some their successful coping strategy throughout life is to adopt a leadership position and to forge forward, hopefully taking others with them. Others may adopt a position as follower preferring not to be in the front line. However, it does not mean that by taking a follower position one cannot lead. In fact many good leaders seek out the opinions of others, empower others and lead from the back. If through good active listening we can identify an individual's preferred coping strategy and behaviour pattern we can make sure that these preferences fit the work assigned to them. In this way we increase the likelihood of the person being happy and more productive in their post.

Using emotions

Human beings are, by their very nature, emotional. We are never without emotions, even when we are trying hard to be or appear unemotional. Think of all the emotions we experience in the course of just one day. The felt emotions provide the backcloth of our actions. They will colour the way we think and respond to things. We may come into work in an emotional state which changes our response to what we encounter or we may be confronted with something which changes our emotional state. Increasingly, the business world is coming to value and seek out emotionally intelligent leaders. It is no longer expected or accepted that leadership is a purely rational activity in which emotions are obstacles. Emotional intelligence is now a prerequisite for most organisations when choosing their leaders. In order to communicate well one has to understand one's own emotions and those of others. Organisations continually need to deal with emotionally challenging situations – relentless change, increasing expectations and a constant striving for limited resources.

All of these concerns can raise strong emotions, as our physical realm/*Umwelt* feels under threat in a very concrete way if we fear that we will not have the finances to provide for ourselves and our families. At the same time it reminds us of the uncertainty of our existence – we cannot expect things to continue forever; it attacks our sense of self, making us feel vulnerable and lost – if I lose my job, who will I be, how will I identify myself? This is destabilising to our psychological dimension/*Eigenwelt*. Equally, the thought of the organisation failing can also attack our sense of purpose and meaning (spiritual dimension/*Uberwelt*) – what and who shall I follow, why will I get up each morning? It also reduces our opportunities for being with others (social dimension/*Mitwelt*) and leads to emotions such as loneliness and isolation. Indeed, 'emotions are important because if we did not have them, nothing else would matter ... Emotions are the stuff of life ... The most important bond or the glue that links us together' (Elster 1999, p. 403).

Contrary to some older leadership theories, suppressing emotions is bad for business. You may think it's best to ignore emotions in tough business situations, but there are two big problems with this tactic. It's hard to do, and more importantly, it's not in your interest to do so. An awareness of the emotions of our workforce allows us to understand our organisation. People have come to understand that emotions do not just 'appear', they are always intentional, they are always directed towards and about 'something'. Awareness of people's emotions offers insight into what is going well and what isn't, and points us in the direction of how to make it better. If we ignore what the emotions are telling us and don't address the situation it causes dissatisfaction and 'negative' emotions. These will build, and employees have a limited number of potential responses. They may choose to leave. They may feel disengaged from the organisation and reduce their work effort or the quality of their work, and absenteeism may increase. They may be loyal but feel disempowered and just patiently wait for the situation to improve. If the environment is an open one which values dialogue they may have a more positive response and use their voices to address their emotions and concerns with the hope of changing the situation. This departs from earlier leadership models where leaders have been encouraged to hide their humanity and model a more rational and unemotional approach. By addressing those concerns proactively, you can steer a potentially negative conversation to a positive place and thus extract greater cooperation from your superiors, colleagues and those reporting to you.

We have noted the growth in companies acknowledging the importance of emotions and seeking 'emotionally intelligent' leaders. The foci of emotional intelligence fit neatly alongside existential concerns (see Table 6.1). Both require the leader to know who they are – to know their emotional strengths and weaknesses, including triggers which may affect their emotional response.

A leader who can recognise emotions and not hide from them is a much more effective leader. Such a leader will be experienced as more insightful and caring and therefore worthy of trust. Many different emotions arise in everyday personal and professional communications. These can be emotions attached to the joy and fulfilment of a project finished well or equally more difficult ones linked to conflicts stemming from a number of predictable core concerns:

- Appreciation (recognition of value)
- Affiliation (emotional connection to others)
- Autonomy (freedom to feel, think, or decide)
- Status (standing compared with others)
- Role (job label and related activities).

These all relate to our self-concept and related existential concerns – freedom, relatedness, anxiety etc. By addressing those emotional concerns proactively, you can steer a potentially negative conversation to a positive place and engender greater cooperation.

As you promote and model emotional intelligence in your organisation, you will get more value out of the good times and do a better job of overcoming the bad. Using an emotionally intelligent approach, which addresses the emotional needs of colleagues, makes it more likely that they will feel a sense of belonging and commitment. Emotional wellbeing in the workplace increases if we feel that our emotions are important to those around us, particularly our leaders.

As I have outlined earlier, most current leadership models now start with the assumption that a leader must demonstrate emotional intelligence. This is an acceptance that the very act of leadership is a relational one. It is dependent on the leader having followers and therefore on a human relationship. Involvement in a human relationship of any kind is relational and therefore emotional.

The understanding of emotions, both our own and those of others, is key to the development of emotional literacy from which one can develop emotional resilience. How to develop authentic emotional resilience in yourself and

Table 6.1 Emotional intelligence domains and competences linked to existential issues

EMOTIONAL INTELLIGENCE		EXISTENTIAL
	personal competences – how we manage ourselves	
Self Awareness	***Emotional self awareness*** Reading one's own emotions and recognising their impact; using 'gutsense' to guide decisions.	All of these fits within the psychological dimension – **Eigenwelt**.
	Accurate self-assessment Knowing one's strengths and limitations	The focus being our relationship to self. They also require self-awareness of bodily sensation and an understanding of what our body is telling us – **Umwelt**
	Self-confidence Having a sound sense of one's self-worth and capabilities	This fits in **Eigenwelt**
Self Management	***Emotional self-control*** Keeping disruptive emotions and impulses under control	This also fits in the **Eigenwelt** dimension, relating to the importance placed on emotions in the Existential approach. When working existentially emotions are regarded as a welcome tool which provide a gateway to understanding a person's values and beliefs
	Transparency Displaying honesty, integrity, and trustworthiness	**Authenticity** is an important aspect of the existential approach. Leaders are required to be open and honest in order to build trust. Transparency is regarded as a positive attribute but should not be an excuse to not shoulder the responsibility which is central in a leadership role.
	Adaptability Demonstrating flexibility in adapting to changing situations or overcoming obstacles	Flexibility may be required in relation to a number of the existential dimensions. There may need to be flexibility about the physical aspects of the workspace – hot-desking, home working etc. **Umwelt**; the relational aspects –how we work with colleagues **Mitwelt**; flexibility in thinking **Eigenwelt**

EMOTIONAL INTELLIGENCE		*EXISTENTIAL*
	Achievement Having the drive to improve performance to meet inner standards of excellence	**Drive** fits in the **Eigenwelt** but is driven by our values **Uberwelt**
	Initiative Being ready to act and to seize opportunities	Although mainly concerned with **Eigenwelt** it has to be considered in relation to others and their ability to embrace or disrupt the initiative – **Mitwelt**
	Optimism Seeing the positive in events.	This fits mainly within the **Eigenwelt** and **Uberwelt** but the existential calls for an authentic assessment which is neither optimist or pessimistic

EI		*EXISTENTIAL*
	Social competences – how we manage relationships	
Social Awareness	*Empathy* Sensing other's emotions, understanding their perspectives, and taking active interest in their concerns	In order to be empathic one has to first know oneself **Eigenwelt**, and then to open oneself up to the potentiality of understanding others **Mitwelt**
	Organisational awareness Reading the currents, decision networks, and politics at organisational level	This sits primarily within the **Eigenwelt** but must hold an understanding of others **Mitwelt**, an awareness of physical factors **Umwelt** and of values **Uberwelt**
	Service Recognising and meeting follower, client, or customer needs	Although essentially in relation to others **Mitwelt** these needs may be physical **Umwelt**, psychological **Eigenwelt** or value led – **Uberwelt**
Relationship Management	*Inspirational Leadership* Guiding and motivating with a compelling vision	This section sits primarily in relationship to others so therefore in **Mitwelt**, However, inspirational leaders use all the dimensions to create and communicate to others an inspiring value led vision - **Uberwelt**

EMOTIONAL INTELLIGENCE		EXISTENTIAL
	Influence Using a range of tactics for persuasion	Although existential leaders would probably not embrace the idea of 'persuasion' they would seek to use EI and consideration of all the dimensions to create a vision and goal which contained acknowledgement of all needs. This inclusiveness is in itself attractive and thus persuasive.
	Developing others Bolstering others' abilities through feedback and guidance	Transformative leadership places the development of others at its heart. This focuses on **Mitwelt** but has to include psychological connection **Eigenwelt** and an understanding of any physical **Umwelt** needs and values **Uberwelt**.
	Change catalyst Initiating, managing, and leading in a new direction	Conflict is all about perceptions **Eigenwelt** yet always relational **Mitwelt** and often triggered by misunderstanding or different values and priorities - **Uberwelt**
	Conflict management Resolving disagreements	Conflict is all about perceptions **Eigenwelt** yet always relational **Mitwelt** and often triggered by misunderstanding or different values and priorities - **Uberwelt**
	Building bonds Cultivating and maintaining a web of relationships	Building bonds Cultivating and maintaining a web of relationships
	Team work and collaboration Fostering cooperation and team building	We need to take note of the need for belonging and social interaction and connectedness **Mitwelt** but not lose sight of individual physical and psychological needs **Umwelt & Eigenwelt** and basing the shared connection on shared values - **Uberwelt**

others is probably something for another book, but it is now an essential requirement in any work context and an essential skill for any leader. If we learn to listen to the noesis, then we are beginning to listen to the emotions. We learnt earlier that people are never without emotions, but the emotional context of what people say is often overlooked by the listener. This may be due to lack of skill or may stem from a fear of meeting a charged expression of emotion. In understanding a person's emotional stance we gain an entry to their worldview and are helped to interact more effectively and empathically with them. Having one's own emotions noticed and noted may be a rare luxury which allows an individual to feel heard and seen. It is not fluffy or irrelevant for a leader to take note of and work with the emotions; it builds a richer, and ultimately more realistic and trusting, working relationship which will aid creativity and authentic relating.

Using the existential dimensions

I introduced the idea of the four existential dimensions earlier and have referred to them throughout the book. An existential leader may use these as a way of reflecting on their own 'being-in-the-workplace' as a leader. It can be enlightening also to check this outside of the business or organisational context in your day-to-day existence. You may identify one or more of the dimensions which are undeveloped or non-existent and as a result may wish to give them some attention. You may also identify that you are in conflict between one dimension and another. One example of this type of dimensional conflict may be an identification that time and temporality are of great importance to you. You recognise that life is short and temporary. You want to make life a fully lived experience embracing all the existential dimensions. However, how this knowledge is played out in the work context may be paradoxical. The time one gives to work can be at the detriment of your relationship with others (*Mitwelt*) and yourself (*Eigenwelt*). Equally, you may be looking to the work environment to fulfil your needs in all the dimensions. It is important that whichever it is, this is identified, but there is no expectation or requirement that once an imbalance or tension is identified that you must seek to change the balance – you need just to note it and take responsibility for change or no change.

Using the dimensions as a framework for listening and structured thinking can also help leaders in exploring the worldview of others, leading to a more complete (though never fully complete) idea of their values, beliefs, skills and passions. It allows us a structure to ensure that we take note of all the aspects which make each of us unique. We can build a new vision of an individual in their working life based on the four dimensions, which will allow us to consider some key aspects:

- Complexity of individual
- Search for coherence and meaning

- Search for harmonious understanding of organisation/company and employee
- Shared dilemmas
- Coping with death/endings (physical, redundancy, vision, concepts, status, hope)
- Maintaining integrity.

If we succeed it doing that, the individual will feel both seen and heard. When we feel holistically taken note of in this way we feel respected and trusted and are inclined to feel more trusting and respectful toward the other person, placing us in a better position to form a positive working collaboration based on respect and trust. If we feel trusted this gives us the confidence to be open, creative and developmental, an asset to the team and the organisation.

When emotions are positively noted, so is our humanity. We are not being treated as a commodity, or part of the machinery, but as unique individuals with thoughts and feelings.

We can also use the dimensions as a way of checking our business model. Does it service the four existential dimensions of our staff team and the community and environment in which our organisation sits? I have mapped this onto the diagram of the dimensions in Figure 6.1.

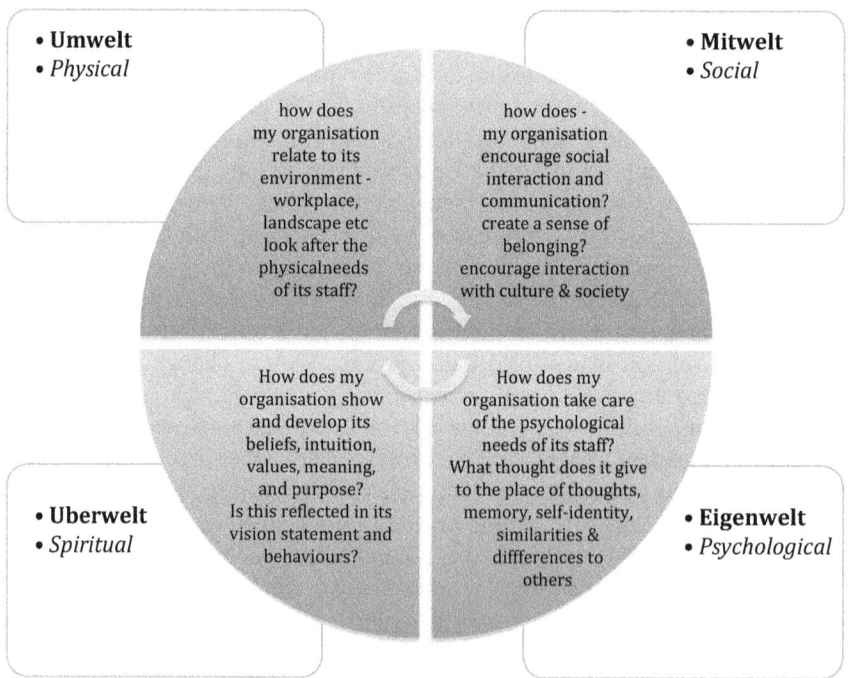

Figure 6.1 Existential dimensions in organisations

This may raise a number of questions in relation to each of the dimensions.

How do you work with the needs of the *Umwelt*? In what ways do you consider the needs of staff, self, organisation and community in relation to the *physical dimension*? This may include the geographical aspect and how your building fits into the natural landscape – (does it enhance or damage the land?), the physical comfort and attractiveness of the workplace, the space which each individual has available, light, heat, the way any physical disability in your team is treated, etc.

How do you work with the needs of the *Mitwelt*? In what ways do you consider the needs of staff, self, organisation and community in relation to the *social dimension*? How do you work reflectively when considering the relational needs of your staff team? Do you want to incorporate space and time for social interaction? Do you want your organisation to be part of the local community and to interact with it or to be a standalone business etc.?

How do you work with the needs of the *Uberwelt*? In what ways do you consider needs in relation to the *spiritual dimension*. In what ways do your vision and mission statements reflect your organisation's values and beliefs? How are these demonstrated in practice? How do you take heed of the needs of each individual to find meaning in their work?

How do you work with the needs of the *Eigenwelt*? In what ways do you consider needs in relation to the *psychological dimension*? This picks up on the psychological need for meaning and belonging. How does your organisation look after the psychological wellbeing of those working within it?

By working through the core concepts and the four dimensions one can gain a better understanding of oneself, others, one's context and how they all interrelate. The skills needed to do this form part of the emotional intelligence of a leader. The goals for your further development will flow through all of the existential dimensions and form the baseline for your vision and mission statements, which in turn need to be congruent with your actions and ways of being.

Chapter 7

Four ages of existential leadership

We have seen that an existential leadership model will hold at its heart the search for meaning and the authentic holding of values. For many leaders there will be times when personal values and organisational values are in conflict, leading to feelings of inauthenticity and bad faith. There will be challenges in the ways they relate to others, and the ways they relate to the context in which their leadership role sits. To be authentic, there will be confrontation with uncertainty at every point but a willingness to use this uncertainty creatively and take responsibility for the outcome. These aspects are present whether a person is new to leadership or approaching retirement as a leader. Leadership is not a static state.

People move through many stages in their management and leadership careers. Each leadership phase may focus on different existential dilemmas and challenges. In 2014, I worked with Jamie Reed on identifying four stages of leadership which track the journey of the existential leader from operational manager through to senior leader; then CEO, MD and Chair to retired and non-executive director. I believe it is worth briefly considering the particular existential challenges which each stage may present. As we are all unique, the personal existential challenges will differ from one individual to another.

The newly promoted operational manager/team leader

Possible key existential issues prior to promotion: frustration and existential anxiety about future development.

Promotion to the role of Operational Manager is often received, in the UK at least, as a consequence of demonstrating excellence at an operational level. From an existential perspective prior to promotion an employee at this level is likely to experience a comparatively limited sense of uncertainty around their role and function, whilst perhaps experiencing some anxiety about future career paths. In relation to their tasks, they believe that they know what they are doing. They are generally told by someone else what they need to do, how to do it and by when. They have accrued potentially thousands of hours of practice in that role. If they are in line for promotion they should have received positive feedback, confirming that the way they are working is in line with, or possibly even exceeds, expectation. The certainty they hold about ways of doing things may in fact be well placed. As a consequence, even in times of considerable uncertainty in their respective market, they may experience limited existential anxiety focused on performance compared to when they started in the role.

In addition they may experience secondary 'gains' such as strong sense of identity at work, increased self-confidence and higher self-esteem as a result of being good at their job. For a time this experience may keep an individual from a sense of temporal uncertainty around their future. The individual's past experience and strong record of success may shield them somewhat from the anxiety of an uncertain future and their abilities in a different role.

So uncertainty may not be a major concern until the possibility and/or desire for promotion to a management or leadership role presents itself. As well as the opportunity to make more money and to find new challenges by gaining greater influence and power in the organisation, it can lead to false assumptions that they will be more in control of life. Finding that this isn't the case can create anxiety.

Any promotion requires a change of function and the acquisition of new skills. This means spending less time in operational delivery and more time leading or managing. Initially this phase is akin to an ironic game of existential snakes and ladders. In the desire to experience more control, more success and greater certainty, we must first expose ourselves to greater uncertainty and more anxiety by confronting what we don't know about our new role. Starting in a new post can also raise other potential existential challenges such as questions of authenticity.

- Who am I in this new role?
- What sort of manager do I want to be?
- How will this impact on how I am seen in the organisation?
- How will this impact on how I see myself?
- How will this impact on those close to me, outside of work?

Authenticity and its pursuit in existential terms require taking responsibility for the unique nature of our being. This includes the capacity to attempt to be true to one's self. Prior to achieving any sort of management position, it can be relatively easy to behave in a way that will be pleasing to others and so help gain promotion. This may be known colloquially as 'playing the game'. Sartre (1966) was very interested in playing and 'being in a way' as a strategy for avoiding facing uncertainty, and the knowledge of our 'nothingness'. This was through acting out a part, 'being' in the way that we perceive others to 'be' in the same role. However, when promoted, we accept a greater degree of responsibility and accountability for our actions. This responsibility in turn can disclose our anxiety and call us to question our authenticity.

This can represent a real challenge for people. Initially this uncertainty can represent a period of isolation and limited sense of safety. It may help to offer a real example of someone in this leadership stage and the way in which the existential issues manifested themselves. This acts as an example of the way the existential dimensions and issues are evident in leadership and the paradoxes we, as leaders, may be faced with by placing them in a concrete situation.

When working as a coach for a large organisation I saw these issues very clearly in my work with Steve. Steve's situation reminded me of Kierkegaard's (1989, p. 57) statement that 'The most common form of despair is not being who you are'. Steve had worked for the organisation for many years in a number of different posts. A year previously, he had moved from managing a small autonomous unit where he had led a small team of mainly part-time staff to a new position where he became the team leader and manager of a larger team of full-time workers, each of whom managed their own teams of part-time workers. The members of his new team were geographically distant from each other and under their previous manager had complained of poor communication from leaders, leaving them feeling 'out of the loop'. They were suspicious of management and felt unsupported. Some of the team had worked for the organisation for a long time and had known Steve in his previous post where he had been at the same level as them and had at times joined in the complaints about the leadership and management teams. They had conflicting feelings about Steve's promotion. On one hand they resented being 'abandoned' by him 'joining the other side', yet also felt that they would get better treatment and understanding from Steve as he knew what it was like to do their jobs.

On our first meeting, Steve came across as a large, confident man in his late forties. I noticed that he dressed very formally in suit and tie, although this was by no means the norm for the organisation, which had a very liberal dress code. He was warm and welcoming but at the same time I experienced him as tense and worried and at times his hands shook. He told me that he had enjoyed his previous work, feeling confident in his abilities to lead his small team, believing that he was a good team player, knowledgeable, skilled and well liked. He saw himself as 'a working class guy made good, a bit on the macho side ... in many ways, one of the lads'. He had enjoyed building his previous team of part-timers through a mixture of regular 'teambuilding' social events, several taking place in the pub, partnered with a quite directive management style.

He had applied for his current leadership position because he felt that as a man he was expected to show ambition and not seem apathetic. He also saw younger and, to his eyes, 'less skilled' men applying for and gaining promotion and he believed he could do a better job than them or the previous postholder. In addition, he was also feeling left behind by his wife who held a very senior position in industry where she earned considerably more money than he did. His wife was keen to take early retirement and for Steve to 'support her for a change'. He dearly wished to be in a position to do this.

In Steve's relationship to his wife and his colleagues we might see his desire for involvement and intimacy coupled paradoxically with his fear of engulfment (Sartre, Laing) encompassing a terror of being smothered, taken over and losing his autonomy and freedom. To fight this he was swinging to extremes where at times he tried to control others, separating out himself as manager and leader from the employees, and at other times when he tried hard just to be part of the group again.

We can see some of the paradoxes in Steve's life (Figure 7.1). For Steve, the world provided sufficient paradoxes to throw him into a desperate, depressed and, at the time I saw him, a frozen and petrified state. He was experiencing that Laingian state of insubstantiality, and had lost the ability to assume that the stuff he was made of was genuine, good or valuable.

One of the ontological, universal human shared givens is that contradictions, which are irresolvable, are constantly with us. They can be called instincts, inclination or intuitions. Human beings are thrown into this world to find meaning through aspiring to something and achieving something meaningful which may leave a legacy. At the same time, as soon as we achieve our aspirations we may become bored, exhausted, worn out and apathetic,

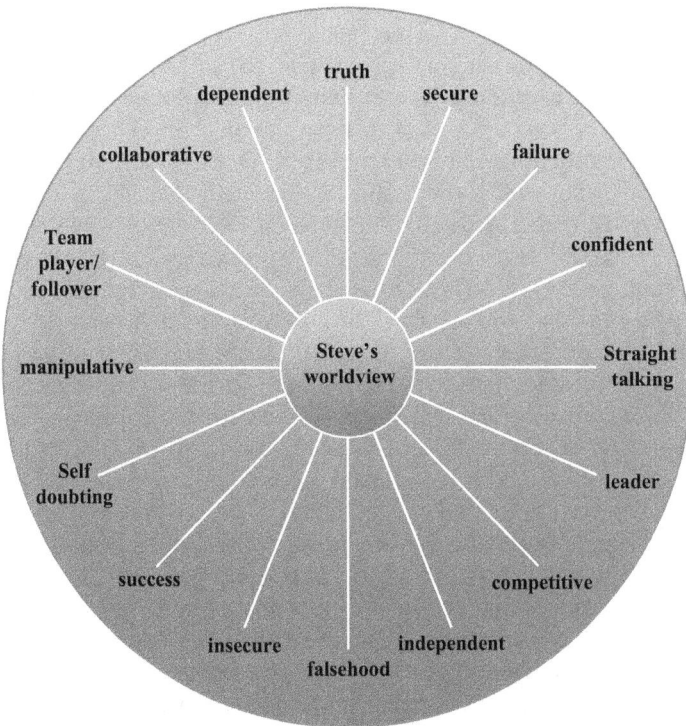

Figure 7.1 Paradoxes in worldview

and understand that new aspirations need to be created. These states of being may be accompanied by paradoxes of belonging versus isolation, security versus risk taking, apathy versus ambition, being honest and straightforward versus controlling and manipulative. Steve prided himself in being straightforward and honest so finding himself acting in a more dishonest and complex way was disheartening for him.

Steve was faced with some difficult issues. He needed to come to terms with the knowledge that promotion and a role as leader did not address all his needs and that, as with all decisions we make, there were losses as well as gains. He had to choose what he really valued and to take responsibility for his choice. The contradiction, which Steve struggled with, was how he could have ambition *and* a sense of security and belonging. It seemed that in order to answer the call to be ambitious and successful he was called upon to sacrifice his sense of safety and belonging and experience the isolation of the new. As Strasser and Strasser (1997, p. 69) pointed out, the need for humans to engage in a 'perennial search for safety and security in a world that is replete with uncertainties and unpredictability is one of the paradoxes of our existence'. This was certainly so in Steve's case.

At this stage of his career, Steve had taken a risk in attaching himself to the ambitious polarity, which very much supported his sense of self-worth as a grown man supporting his wife and children. However, he paid a price in losing the sense of belonging he had experienced in his relationship with his colleagues and the workforce. He was flung head first into a well of loneliness. He also found his own self-image to be attacked, with his colleagues seeing him very differently from how he saw himself. This was terrifying for Steve as it attacked his whole self-concept and left him with a feeling of obliteration. In some ways he had ceased to be.

Having succeeded in his aspiration to move upwards on the career ladder, he felt afraid, guilty and desirous to move back to his old familiar secure self. However he knew that the security had previously brought with it feelings of boredom and apathy, leaving him remorseful, self-denigrating and wanting to move to a more autonomous and ambitious self. His coping mechanisms, both in his employment and his intimate life, alternated between cooperation and competition in relation to his colleagues and to his wife. His background had prepared him to be the dominant partner in marriage. Yet he found himself drawn to an independent, confident and successful woman of whom he was to some degree in awe, leaving him fluctuating between behaving submissively towards her or trying to assert his superiority and masculinity through the workplace and an attempt to match his wife's salary.

Another paradox also came into play: success versus failure. In his previous position he was considered successful, but in his new position he began to see that he was now viewed as a failure. Senior managers were beginning to make complaints about him; grievances and disciplinaries were becoming regular occurrences. His team reported concerns including that he did not understand or communicate the national policies, was unsupportive to his staff, some of whom felt bullied by him. He was perceived as competitive towards the men he managed and condescending towards the women. These perceptions were in total conflict to Steve's values and to how he saw himself and wanted to be seen by others. Some of the complaints also focused on the ways in which Steve criticised other members of the leadership team and offered personal information about other leaders to those he was managing. The team considered much of his behaviour to be manipulative and dishonest, trying to be their 'friend' one minute and being critical and dictatorial the next. Team members questioned what he might say about them behind their backs. This really challenged Steve's view of himself as he viewed this same behaviour as being honest and straight talking and as being part of the team. It also made it hard for him to become a full member of the leadership team as his comments about individuals in that team were leaked. He was left in no man's land.

His working relationship with his team completely broke down and it was at this point that his firm arranged for Steve to have three coaching sessions to explore these issues and to identify strategies to improve the situation. His 'superior self', with which he had previously been very well acquainted, had all but disappeared and his self-esteem had plummeted. He found himself behaving in ways which were fundamentally opposed to his values and self-concept. It was difficult for Steve to see that whilst he prided himself on being a cooperative 'team player' he was experienced as being competitive. His sense of belonging was challenged.

Through existential coaching Steve was able to explore his worldview, the ways in which he was behaving, and the paradoxical relationship this behaviour appeared to have with his value system. Steve felt most safe in his relationship to his own body and the *Umwelt*, the physical world of objects and environment. In this dimension Steve felt at home in his male body most of the time, he loved rugby and sessions in the local gym. He took pleasure in the physical power of his body. He enjoyed the way that his strength allowed him to offer help to others, particularly women. He was well known for being the person who would carry cases, move tables etc. He was also very aware that he valued the potential for violence which his powerful body allowed. Although he did not get into physical fights it was important for him to feel that he had the physical measure of another man and the belief that he would win in a physical fight. Yet he talked painfully of his experience of an accident, which had left him temporarily with a shattered arm leaving him dependent on others for many basic tasks. His need to be both leader and helper (social dimension) were challenged by the injury and the physical and emotional vulnerability he could not ignore. He began to explore the temporality of his strong body and the paradoxical relationship which he had with it. The coaching enabled him to see himself as both a potential helper and a potential fighter. His body could lead him to feel powerful or vulnerable. It was in a constant state of change and would not always remain strong and would eventually cease to exist.

However, for Steve, it was the social dimension (*Mitwelt*), the world of other people, where he found his most challenging contradiction – his need to belong and the possibility of isolation. His ambition to do well in his career and match his wife's achievements resulted in him leaving a safe and satisfying social group. In that group he felt he belonged, was liked and respected, could have a laugh and a joke, did well and felt confident. In entering another social group, made up of leaders and managers, instead of feeling good about himself through his increased salary and movement up the professional hierarchy, his self-esteem plummeted. He felt isolated and alone, he lost his sense of fun and felt he was heading for depression. In his new social world it was considered to be beneath him to move tables and carry boxes. He was expected to 'beat' his colleagues through his knowledge and intelligence, not his physical strength. The kudos his strong body had gained for him in the past was of no consequence here. He found it hard to form relationships within the new leadership group. He struggled to find a 'common language' and longed to be back in his previous post where he could again be one of the boys and 'feel more like his real self'. This desire was in direct conflict with his wish to be seen as more competent and 'better' than his previous colleagues and for this to be acknowledged through his promotion.

Through the coaching Steve reengaged with his power and identified the fact that he had made choices. He did not have to apply for his present position; he had chosen to do so. In doing so he had focused on his ambition and his need to feel equal to his wife. He had ignored what would be lost if he achieved this. He could now review and take responsibility for his choice. He was not stuck with it. His managers were keen to keep Steve in the company. He had proved himself to be an excellent worker in his previous post. However, as Steve was beginning to realise, he could not have everything and needed to have a clear sense of who he was in order to move on.

For Steve it proved a difficult task to decide what was most important to him and what would allow him to regain his self-esteem and sense of authentic living. He considered who he believed himself to be and who he truly was. He engaged with his transience and his own potentialities. What he wanted and needed at twenty may have become 'sedimented' in his mind, causing him tension and no longer being meaningful in his forties. We explored the potential to stir some of his sedimentations. Strasser, Spinelli and van Deurzen all stress the importance of re-examining these sedimented values and emotions to check out their meaning and validity in the immediate situation.

In the exploration of Steve's *Eigenwelt*, we focused on his personal psychological dimension, his inner world, helping him explore his paradoxes and the tension between integrity and disintegration. This included looking at the assumptions he held about what he felt his wife needed him to be, what he believed he needed to be to match his perceived responsibilities to his wife and how he felt others judged him in relation to her professional success. These were challenging areas but he engaged with the challenge and saw that he held many assumptions which he had never checked. This led to him having a conversation with his wife where he openly shared his feeling of inadequacy in relation to her and his struggle to address this through promotion at work. Both saw that he was not yet clear whether his need to fulfil his ambition was more important than his need to belong. His wife was clear that she was tired of her own professional struggle and wanted to take early retirement within the next five years in order for them to spend more time together and for her to re-engage with who she truly believed herself to be. She also felt he owed it to her as recompense for his previous affair.

As we have seen, the *Uberwelt*, or spiritual dimension, provides a place where we seek to find meaning against the threat of meaninglessness. For Steve it was clearly an important and hidden one – a world in which his paradoxes were very evident. Steve confided in me that he carried round a small notebook in which he wrote poetry. He shared his writings with very few people, none of whom were in his working environment. His poetry was sensitive, clearly showing his love of the beauty of the physical world and it provided a framework for him to explore his philosophical relationship to the world, particularly ethical dilemmas focusing on his sense of justice. This dimension was not evident in the way he was living his life at home or at work. The limited time we had available meant we were not able to explore this dimension very fully but we gave it the respect and importance which it deserved, so that Steve was able to accept it as an important part of his being. Steve was able to realise and become aware of his limitations and possibilities in terms of the human givens and re-engage with his ability to choose. He was able to find a more authentic way of being in his role as manager, team leader and husband. He learned that he could not expect to get all his emotional needs met through his team and in his new position he had to move on from being 'one of the boys' and address Rollo May's (1999) paradox of freedom versus responsibility.

For Steve, exploring his own experience of the Heideggerian concept of 'thrownness' allowed him the opportunity to consider his own autonomy and the ability to be perceived as behaving authentically. He was able to accept his own vulnerabilities and recognise them as potential strengths, understanding Sartre's concept that as human beings we pretend that we share a solidity with objects and in seeking security turn from our fear of fundamental nothingness and reinvent ourselves in bad faith, denying our freedom and ability to choose (Sartre 1966). He was able to examine some of his more paradoxical behaviours and to honestly consider who he was and what he wanted, at the same time noting the apparent contradictions, and the limitations in any decision. In order to get something – promotion – he would lose something – social belonging.

Steve decided to remain in the leadership role and to put his energy into developing new social networks outside of work. He took up opportunities for training. I could not help feeling a little sad as I felt he had opted, like

Sartre's waiter, to take on the uniform of leader rather than to authentically be his own kind of leader and I later learnt that when the company restructured he chose to return to a more operational role.

The senior leader/manager seeking directorship

Possible key existential issues: isolation, authenticity, self-esteem, freedom and responsibility

This is the next step on the leadership ladder. The individual will have developed considerable industry relevant management experience, performing and delivering to the highest level. Over the preceding years it is likely that they may have experienced a number of interim promotions before reaching a senior leader role. The key indicator of this position is the move away from any operational delivery. This shift means work is now primarily strategic, aimed at determining, communicating and implementing the organisational focus and development. The move away from an established area of expertise and experience can have a negative impact on self-esteem and confidence. There may be changes in the type of language that is being used at this level, indicative of the change of focus from operational to strategic. This may feel like a move to a foreign country with a different language. This is evidenced in the case study of Steve I have already referred to, leading to feelings of isolation.

At this level, the leader's decisions are likely to have far-reaching, possibly profound, strategic and financial implications for the organisation and the individuals in it. As a consequence, the leader has a greater level of visibility and responsibility for decisions and their outcomes.

Given the potential size of the team that a senior leader is likely to be responsible for, their core contact with operational delivery is probably through department heads. This engagement is one step away from those delivering the work. It changes relationships. The higher the level of responsibility for making high level decisions, the less direct contact leaders have with those who will be directly impacted by the decisions being made.

Almost inevitably leaders at this level will be required to present to the Board. This in itself can require a unique set of skills that may well be new to the individual. Being able to communicate effectively and authentically, and therefore add value, can be pivotal for future promotions. At this stage in the life of a leader the existential question of authenticity may become more central. Board Directors are responsible for the direction of the business and not the operational delivery. A senior manager reporting to the board, even if they have a predominantly overseeing role, is still far more connected to the day-to-day delivery. The level of knowledge that is needed for a senior leader or manager is far greater than for a Board Director. A Board Director may be future focused while the senior leader has to hold the tension between what is needed in the moment and its relationship to future goals. This requires a senior leader to navigate between the immediacy of the production line and the future oriented board, whilst remaining true and authentic in both contexts. They may hold knowledge from both groups and have to make sensitive decisions about what needs to be shared and how that is done.

This is a time when a senior leader may feel caught in the middle and quite isolated. When I was at this level I experienced such a tension when the organisation was planning a restructure. As a member of the senior leadership team I was aware that redundancies had to be made and it was my job, together with three other senior leaders, to decide where the savings should come from. After difficult discussions we decided, as a group of four, that the best place to take the cuts was at our level and we wrote a paper proposing that the four posts be cut to two, each of which would cover two geographical areas and more responsibility. The confidential papers requesting us to decide on redundancies were stolen from the bag of one of the group. The papers contained the proposal to make the cuts at management and leadership level but did not name posts. We were faced with a very angry middle management team who assumed that we would not take cuts at our own level but would look to their level. We had agreed with the Board not to discuss anything at this stage so although we knew that all middle management posts were safe we could not give them this information and instead had to listen to all manner of accusations and abuse. Perhaps the worst thing was knowing that we were not trusted to make a thoughtful and value-led decision and that we could no longer trust members of the middle management team as one had gone into the personal bag of a senior manager to take the papers. We had to accept that we were seen differently by those working to us, and by those we worked to.

At this level a leader has to ask:

- How am I now seen in the organisation?
- How does this change how I see myself?
- How do I remain authentic and aligned to my values?
- How do I hold the tension of being 'in the middle'?

The CEO, MD, Chairman

Possible key existential issues: isolation, uncertainty, disappointment, authenticity

At the start of a corporate career, reaching the CEO level may be seen as the ultimate objective. However, when you consider the basic pyramid structure of organisations you are quickly left with the reality that there are more employees than CEOs, so many individuals will be disappointed. In addition, when you consider the three key traits of a CEO as described by Justin Menkes (2011) in the *Harvard Business Review* blog we are presented with a set of very interesting personality traits:

1   Realistic Optimism: the capacity to have confidence to pursue audacious goals without self-delusion and in full awareness of the magnitude of the challenges
2   Subservience to Purpose: so much so that their goal is 'their master and their reason for being'.
3   Finding Order in Chaos: the ability to find multi-dimensional problem solving invigorating.

Let us consider each of these individual elements in turn from an existential perspective. The position of *realistic optimism* is going to require the individual to believe that they have achieved mastery of managing existential uncertainty in combination with a very clear sense of what is meaningful (authentic) for them. Being very goal orientated requires the ability to sit comfortably with the uncertainty of the future in balance while still being sufficiently grounded in the present to assess what is going on in the moment. However, as is so often the case, with all our choices and abilities, from an existential perspective, there is always the shadow or cost of those choices or abilities. In this context this comes in the form of the cost to the CEO of the things they didn't choose and the capabilities that they didn't develop as a consequence of their dedication to their singularity of purpose. This is an example of Menkes' necessity to have *subservience to purpose* as the pursuit of the goal is the 'reason for being' of the CEO. Whether this enables a balancing of the existential dimensions is a matter for each CEO to consider. This determination and single-mindedness may make it hard for them to see value in relationships with people who don't share their vision and goals. This limits creativity and self-development and may result in isolation. A CEO is often seen as a 'different' kind of being, in some way a superior being who holds knowledge, confidence and certainty. We have seen earlier in this book how humans choose to have, and to use, leaders as a way of passing on responsibility and gaining false certainty. This may create problems for a CEO in terms of their worldview and self-esteem.

With a perceived level of mastery and way of being that often looks to successful problem solving as the primary way of finding meaning there is a lot of scope for a CEO to see everything as a transactional problem to solve. This can be a challenging perspective when in a relationship, unless you share a similar vision. If it is the only mechanism for finding meaning in life, the self-esteem of the CEO can in turn be quite fragile when goals aren't clear or others do not validate decisions.

The retired/non-exec

Possible key existential issues: time and temporality, isolation, self-identity

The experience and circumstance of retirement for employees are always unique. The inevitable shared experience, though, is an experience of an ending. For some this can be a stark confrontation with some large, long unaddressed questions. It is very possible to complete an entire working career without bringing that experience into question before the prospect of retirement forces the issue into consciousness. The working day, week, year and life can be lost in transaction – lost in the doing. As discussed earlier, moving up the management chain is seen as the primary objective for many employees. So, we need to ask ourselves – where do we go, what do we do, when one has no more rungs on the ladder?

There are two core questions at this 'ending' stage. What was my working career for? And, what do I do now? As we have considered, from an existential perspective, endings in their anticipation and manifestation represent the key frame of reference of making meaning of our lives, both in terms of what has gone before, and what we look to do next. Unfortunately, for many, the anxiety and responsibility these endings represent can be overwhelming. A life spent in avoidance of endings can be seen as an attempt to avoid the ultimate end.

Retirement may represent one of the greatest endings that we experience in our lives, short of our physical ending in death. It is, after all, the death of our working life, our most consistent long-standing activity of our adult lives and for many the arena which provides the core of their self-identity – the lives we live at work, the 'community' we 'belong' to there and choose to locate ourselves in. Thus what we 'do' (in the professional capacity) is often seen as a key part of our identity. At parties and meetings the first question is often about what we do (by which people tend to mean 'what is your occupation?'). People may take from that a whole load of assumptions about what social class we belong to, how much we are likely to earn, how intelligent we are and from those assumptions and stereotypes whether they expect us to be like them or alien. This will have a big impact on whether they choose to like us or not.

In addition to the loss of a quick social and possibly personal identifier, retirement brings with it a loss of structure and the loss of the work community. Our careers, in all their forms and phases, provide certain structures which frame our working lives. These structures are usually temporal, hierarchical and motivational. Our working lives are generally bound by temporal requirements constructed around a working day, the length of the working week, the timescale for completion of a project and the amount of annual leave to which we are entitled. It is considered that this time is compensated for and rewarded financially. There exists a simple cause and effect in this relationship. We turn up at an allotted time and complete a series of transactions within given time frames in order to fulfil the terms of our employment contract. Within the organisation there exist further structural givens in the form of the organisational structure and hierarchy. It is as a consequence of these structures that we find a sense of structure and function and a context for motivation and direction. To navigate this successfully after retirement requires an exploration of if, and why structures are important to the individual. If they are deemed to be important then the question which follows has to address what new structures can be put in place to mitigate the loss of those offered through work. The most reliable source of this structure is a clear on-going sense of self and primarily of one's values and beliefs which bring meaning to action.

As leaders approach retirement they are faced with the question as to just what they have achieved during their working life and their leadership and what legacy they will leave behind. For many people the sense of legacy is an important one. Some people consider their children to be their legacies, whilst others seek some lasting recognition for their work achievements. I used to joke that the best way to deal with a difficult leader was to name a building after them, so their 'legacy' was guaranteed and they did not have to make their mark by wholesale changes in order to be noticed and to demonstrate their newfound power.

All legacies are ultimately a denial of our mortality and an attempt to deal with the existential dilemmas of time and temporality. If a legacy is needed then a leader has to consider this earlier in order to lay the foundations. Rather like Dickens' Ghost of Christmas Future in *A Christmas Carol*, on some of my courses I hand out drawings of very elaborate and beautiful tombstones and ask participants to write on them what they would like to see on their tombstones, or to write what they believe their own obituary would say were they to die tomorrow. I follow that by asking them to consider what their 'perfect' obituary would be, how would they like to be remembered? The challenge is then to reflect on what needs to be done differently to ensure that the life lived will result in wording they would enjoy reading and feel proud of. This type of reflection should be present throughout our leadership phases but becomes more crucial as retirement nears. Work and leadership are only phases and markers in our lives, not ways of defining the importance of our existence.

Retirement is not only an ending, but also the beginning of a new phase in life. As with any beginning it needs reflection, work and commitment to make it meaningful. It is a new project, the preparation for which should have started years earlier, but rarely does. One leader may experience it as a surrender of power. For another it may be considered a lifting of responsibility. Whatever the reaction, it throws up another existential question – how will the retired leader use the new freedom and responsibility? Some will transfer the power and responsibility into new arenas. They may take non-executive posts or places of authority in charities or other organisations. Less positively they may transfer their leadership to their family situation and become a dictator, benevolent or otherwise.

For many retirees the existential issue that retirement brings to the fore is that of loneliness. It may have been 'lonely at the top' but they would have been surrounded by people keen to make an impression, to talk with them and to 'be their friend'. Many leaders have neglected their friends and family outside the work environment. Leadership takes a lot of time and energy and can leave some leaders drained for activities outside work. For these, retirement can feel very threatening. They may have to reform relationships with their partners and families. The depths of friendships may need questioning. If work was the only common denominator within the friendship groups then new topics of conversation need to be sought or new friends made. If a leader has been authentic and true to their values and beliefs then this should not be too difficult. Unfortunately many styles of leadership encourage leaders to seek friendship networks whose purpose is to help them up the career ladder, and once a leader is retired they may have little to offer to the group and in turn the group may be of little interest to them.

Chapter 8

Conclusion

Being a leader is both daunting and exhilarating. It provides a canvas for creativity. Yet, it is also a powerful and responsible position to hold. It provides plenty of opportunity to use one's position positively or negatively, knowing that whatever you do will impact on other people. Leaders can disempower or empower the people they work with and need to reflect on the ways in which they use their power. Existentially we might refer to this as 'being-in-leadership-towards-others'. As leaders, and as humans, we are free to act in the way we choose but those choices will have consequences. In a leadership role in a business, those choices will have implications for the leaders, the workforce, the business, customers/clients and shareholders. There is a lot riding on the decisions of the leader.

I trust I have conveyed how urgently I believe we require a new approach to leadership which fits with the concerns of this uncertain century, and what a good fit an existential approach can offer in helping to address the challenges of today. I hope this book also serves to give you some increased understanding of existential leadership and what it means to 'be' an existential leader. In our lives we are sometimes leaders and sometimes followers. They are part of the same cycle. If we think of those arenas in which we take a followership role we will know what we would like from our leaders and so also know what a successful authentic leader looks like. We can consider leaders we have experienced against a set of questions:

- How would we have wanted our leaders to be?
- What values would we have wished them to hold and demonstrate?
- What behaviours would have encouraged us to trust and work with them?
- What could they have done to help us develop?
- Did we experience them as authentic and true to their values and beliefs?

These questions also provide us with a framework to question our own way of being in our leadership roles – are we providing these things for our 'followers'? If we continue to switch our view back and forth from our own perception to a consideration of the possible perceptions of others, we can effectively structure and devise questions for our self-reflective practice.

We have probably all experienced good and bad leaders. I believe we respond most positively to authentic leaders who show an awareness and concern for all aspects of who we are, not just for us as employees or followers, but also as complex and unique individuals who, with a little encouragement, have a lot to offer. It is never nice to experience yourself as being treated like an easily replaceable cog in a wheel. A leader who considers the individual in all the existential dimensions and takes time to understand their values will form a more intense and trusting working relationship than those who don't and will usually form a more successful collaborative partnership.

Of course getting to know and respect someone in this way may make it harder in times of cutbacks and redundancies, but as an informed existential leader you are less likely to let the 'wrong' people go. I have had to face the awful prospect of knowing a person was not achieving, or was in the wrong job, and that the best solution for the organisation was that they moved on. In most cases where I had to take action for the person to leave, knowing something of their worldview, values and aspirations helped. As far as possible I would consider ways in which to enable them to feel empowered to own the problem and to creatively make that move. In some cases I arranged job shadowing or redeployment based on my knowledge of what the individual found meaningful. Many leaders may not consider this part of their role but for me to feel I was acting within my values it was necessary. It was as much for me as for the employee and the organisation. To meet ex-employees whom I had to 'let go' and have them thank me for the way it was done and the appropriateness of the decision is one of a number of the things that I do feel proud of. Most of these people were unhappy in their posts and moved to something more aligned to their interests and skills.

In this book I have attempted to provide an introduction to approaching leadership in an existential way. I have consistently referred back to the existential core concepts and dimensions to show that they can provide a framework for all leadership functions. If we keep them in mind when embarking on our role as an existential leader they can help us to work sensitively and inter-relationally. The model is essentially very simple and yet hard to undertake. The central approach lies in taking respectful notice of others and of ourselves. This is not just to be 'nice', in order to be liked; it is not soft and fluffy. This approach has a strong business leadership function. We may use our better understanding about a person, as a unique individual, to challenge them appropriately for their own development and the development of the organisation. We need also to continually challenge ourselves.

It is this which makes the model difficult because it requires the existential leader to acknowledge that being self-reflective, self-critical, and learning how to be a follower, are important elements of leadership. For many leaders this is a real challenge to the ego. Many images of leaders will show them out at the front with others following, or instructing others what to do. To let go of being centre stage and commanding obedience can make some leaders feel very vulnerable.

Leaders have to constantly change in order to adapt to organisational and societal needs. There will indeed be times when the leader needs to be directive. If a leader is not clear about what needs to be done, then the workforce can feel unsafe and lost. Safety issues may require that some tasks be carried out in the same linear way each time to reduce the risk of accidents. Employment laws and government or organisational policies also need to be followed. Accepting and sharing these 'givens' is part of the authentic nature of existential leadership. Just as we have the concept of 'thrownness' in existential philosophy, there is the equivalent in business. Existential leaders know when to use structure and when to encourage unstructured thinking. They are clear with their staff about what things are changeable and also about what it is not possible to change without disastrous consequences. Some things we can change, others things we have to accept and work with, or decide we are in the wrong place and go elsewhere.

Using an approach which requires the leader to consider social, physical, psychological and spiritual dimensions allows the leader to build a secure bedrock from which an organisation and its staff can embrace change. The workforce will trust a leader who is authentic and honest with them, even about things that are difficult. They will experience existential leaders as 'seeing' and taking an interest in them.

Although I have primarily focused this book around leadership in a business concept, the same existential approach can be applied when we take on leadership roles in other contexts such as being parents or engaging in all manner of projects with others. The same concerns and skills are present no matter what type of leadership is encountered.

If the concepts and philosophy of existential leadership appeal to you, then the challenge is to set about becoming and remaining an existential leader. This is a task you can undertake alone. I have endeavoured to provide a framework for that journey. However, an existential approach holds connectedness and relationship with others at its centre, so I would suggest working with another as the preferred way for aiding self-reflection and self-questioning. I hope that however you structure your journey, along the way you will take time out to ask yourself some of the many questions I have posed as well as those questions which you will identify as pertinent to your own values and needs in your leadership journey.

It is not an easy task to remain an authentic leader working within an existential philosophy but I believe that seeking to do so makes us more aware and gives us the potential to be more effective leaders.

Bibliography

Agapitou V., & Bourantas D., (2017), *Existential Intelligence and Strategic Leadership*, Republic of Moldova: LAP LAMBERT Academic Publishing

Arendt H., (1998), *The Human Condition*, Second Edition, Chicago: University of Chicago Press

Avolio B.J., & Gardner W.L., (2005), Authentic leadership development: Getting to the root of positive forms of leadership, *The Leadership Quarterly* 16(3), 315–338

Bailey, J. (2001). Leadership lessons from Mount Rushmore: An interview with James MacGregor Burns. *Leadership Quarterly*, 12(1), 113–128. http://dx.doi.org/10.1016/S1048-9843(01)00066-2

Becker E., (1973), *The Denial of Death*, New York: Simon & Schuster

Bennis W., (2010), *Still Surprised: A Memoir of a Life in Leadership*, San Francisco: Jossey-Bass

Bennis W.G., and Nanus B. (1997), *Leaders: Strategies for Taking Charge*, New York: Harper Business

Berlin I., (1969), *Four Essays on Liberty*, 1st edition, Oxford: Oxford Paperbacks

Blake R.R., & Mouton S., (1994), *The Managerial Grid*, Houston TX: Gulf Publishing

Blake W., (2002), *Collected Poems*, ed. Yeats W.B., London: Routledge Classics

Boss M., (1963), *Psychoanalysis and Daseinsanalysis*, New York: Basic Books

Boss M., (1994), *Existential Foundations of Medicine and Psychology*, New York: Jason Aronson

Boyatzis R., & McKee A., (2005), *Resonant Leadership: Renewing Yourself and Connecting with Others through Mindfulness, Hope and Compassion*, Cambridge MA: Harvard Business School Press

Camus A., (2000), *The Myth of Sisyphus and Other Essays*, London: Penguin

Camus A., (2013), *The Stranger*, London: Penguin Classics

Canella A.A., & Monroe M.J., (1997), Contrasting perceptions of strategic leaders: towards a more realistic view of top managers, *Journal of Management*, 23(30), 213–230

Cerulo K., (2006), *Never Saw It Coming: Cultural Challenges to Envisioning the Worst*, Chicago: University of Chicago Press

Child J., (1972), Organisational structure, environments and performance: the role of strategic choice, *Sociology*, 6, 47–75

Conger J.A., & Kanungo R.N., (1998), *Charismatic Leadership in Organizations*, Thousand Oaks CA: SAGE publications

Cooper D., (2007), *Psychiatry and Anti-Psychiatry*, ebook, Abingdon:Routledge
Covey S., (2004), *The 7 Habits of Highly Effective People: Powerful Lessons in Personal Change*, New York: Free Press
Cox G. (2009), *How to Be an Existentialist: or How to Get Real, Get a Grip and Stop Making Excuses*, London: Bloomsbury
Csikszentmihalyi M., (1996), *Creativity: Flow and the psychology of discovery and invention*, New York: Harper Collins
Deutsch M., (2000), *The Handbook of Conflict Resolution: Theory and Practice*, Oxford: Wiley
Drucker P., (1996), online interview https://onlinelibrary.wiley.com/doi/abs/10.1002/ltl.40619960306
Elster J., (1999), *Alchemies of the Mind*, Cambridge: Cambridge University Press
Erickson R.J., (1995), The importance of authenticity for self and society, *Symbolic Interaction*, 18(2), 121–144
Finkelstein S., & Hambrick D.C., (1996), *Strategic Leadership: Top Executives and Their Effects on their Organisations*, St Pauls MN: West Publishing
Frankl V.E., (2003), *Man's Search for Meaning*, London: Simon and Schuster
Fromm E., (2001), *The Fear of Freedom*, 2nd ed., London: Routledge
Gardner H., (1983), *Frames of Mind, The Theory of Multiple Intelligences*, New York: Basic Books
Gardner, H., (1999), *Intelligence Reframed: Multiple Intelligences for the 21st Century*, New York: Basic Books
Gardner W.L., & Schermerhorn J.R., (2004), Unleashing individual potential: Performance gains through positive organizational behavior and authentic leadership, *Organizational Dynamics*, 33(3), 270–281
Gardner W.L., Avolio B.J., Luthans F., May D.R., & Walunmbwa F., (2005), 'Can you see the real me?' A self-based model of authentic leader and follower development. *Leadership Quarterly*, 16, 343–372
George B., (2004), *Authentic Leadership: Rediscovering the Secrets to Creating Lasting Value*, Hoboken NJ: John Wiley & Sons
Gill R., (2010), *Theory and Practice of Leadership*, 2nd edition, London: Sage
Goleman D., (1995), *Working with Emotional Intelligence*, London: Bloomsbury
Grant A., (2016), Is 'be yourself' bad advice?, *Psychology Today*, June 2016, online: https://www.psychologytoday.com/gb/blog/happiness-and-the-pursuit leadership/201606/is-be-yourself-bad-advice
Greenleaf R., (1977), *Servant Leadership: A Journey into the Nature of Legitimate Power and Greatness*, New Jersey: Paulist Press
Greenleaf R.K., (2008), *The Servant as Leader*, Westfield IN: Greenleaf Center for Servant Leadership
Greenspan S.I., (1989), Emotional Intelligence, in K. Field, B.J. Cohler, & G. Wool (Eds.), *Learning and Education: Psychoanalytic Perspectives*, Madison, CT: International Universities Press
Hanaway M., & Reed J., (2014), *Existential Coaching Skills: The Handbook*, Henley: CH Group
Hannay A., & Marino G.D. (1998), *The Cambridge Companion to Kierkegaard*, Cambridge: Cambridge University Press
Harary C., & Dagostino M., (2018), *Unlocking Greatness*, USA: Rodale

Harter S., (2002), Authenticity, in C.R. Snyder, & S. Lopez (Eds.), *Handbook of Positive Psychology* (pp. 382–394), Oxford: Oxford University Press
Heidegger M., (1962), *Being and Time*, tr. J. Macquarrie & E. Robinson, Oxford: Blackwell
Hitt M.A., & Tyler B.B., (1991), Strategic decision models: Integrating different perspectives, *Strategic Management Journal*, 12, 327–351
Husserl E., (2009), *The Basic Problems of Phenomenology: From the Lectures, Winter Semester, 1910–1911*, trans. Farin I., & Hart J.G., New York: Springer
Ibarra H., (2015), The authenticity paradox, *Harvard Business Review*, (Jan-Feb).
Jefferson M., (1983), Economic uncertainty and business decision-making, in J. Wiseman (ed.), *Beyond Positive Economics* (pp. 122–159), Proceedings of Section F (Economics) of The British Association for the Advancement of Science (York 1981), London: Macmillan
Jung C.G., (2017), *Psychological Types*, London: Routledge Classics
Kelly J., & Kelly L., (1998) *An Existential-Systems Approach to Managing Organizations*, Westport CT: Quorum Books
Kernis M., (2003), Towards a conceptualization of optimal self-esteem, *Psychological Inquiry* 14(1): 1–26
Kerpen D., (2017), *The Art of People*, London: Penguin Books
Kierkegaard S., (1981), *Kierkegaard's Writings, VIII: Concept of Anxiety: A Simple Psychologically Orienting Deliberation on the Dogmatic Issue of Hereditary Sin*, Princeton: Princeton University Press
Kierkegaard S., (1989), *Sickness Unto Death: A Christian Psychological Exposition of Edification and Awakening by Anti-Climacus*, trans. A. Hannay, London: Penguin Classics
Kierkegaard S., (2009), *Kierkegaard's Writings, XXV: Letters and Documents*, Princeton: Princeton University Press
Kilduff M. & Tsai W., (2003), *Social Networks and Organizations*, London: Sage Publications Ltd
Laing R.D., (1960), *The Divided Self: An Existential Study in Sanity and Madness*, London: Penguin Classics
Laing R.D., (1961), *The Self and Others*, London: Tavistock Publications
Laing R.D., & Cooper D.G., (1971), *Reason and Violence*, New York: Pantheon Books
Lao Tzu, (1973), *Tao Te Ching*, trans. Gia-Fu and Jane English, online, http://peacefulrivers.homestead.com/laotzu.html
Leuner B., (1966), Emotional intelligence and emancipation, *Praxis der Kinderpsychologie und Kinderpsychiatrie*, 15(6), 196–203
Levithan D., (2011), *The Lover's Dictionary*, London: Fourth Estate
Likert R., (1967), *The Human Organization*, New York: McGraw Hill
Lipman-Blumen J., (2000), *Connective Leadership*, Oxford: Oxford University Press
Mandic M., (2012) Authenticity in existential coaching, in E. van Deurzen & M. Hanaway (eds.), *Existential Perspectives in Coaching*, London: Routledge
Marcel G., (1958), *Metaphysical Journal*, tr. B. Wall, London: RockliffMaxwell J.C., (2018), *Developing the Leader within You*, Nashville TN: Harper Collins
May D.R., Chan A.Y.L., Hodges T.D., & Avolio B.J. (2003), Developing the moral component of authentic leadership. *Organizational Dynamics*, 32, 247–260.
May R., (1999), *Freedom and Destiny*, London: Norton

McGregor D., (1968), *Leadership and Motivation Essays*, Cambridge MA: MIT Press

Mengel T., (2008) Learning across games, IVIE Working Paper AD 2007–2005, http://merlin.fae.ua.es/friederike/Dateien/LAGjan09.pdf

Mengel T., (2012), Leading with 'emotional' intelligence – existential and motivational analysis in leadership and leadership development, *Journal on Educational Psychology*, 5(4), 24–31

Menkes J.,(2011), Three traits every CEO needs, *Harvard Business Review*blog,11 May, https://hbr.org/2011/05/three-traits-every-ceo-needs?cm_sp=mos

Merleau-Ponty M., (2013), *Phenomenology of Perception*, Abingdon: Routledge

Musser S.J., (1987), *The Determination of Positive and Negative Charismatic Leadership*, Grantham PA: Messiah College

Nichols R.G., (1980), The Struggle to be Human, Keynote address to First Annual Convention of the International Listening Association, Atlanta, Georgia, 17 February, https://www.listen.org/resources/Nichols%20Struggle%20to%20be%20Human.pdf

Nietzsche F., (1960), *The Will to Power*, tr. Walter Kaufmann & R.J. Hollingdale, New York: Vintage Books (Random House)

Nietzsche F., (2006), *The Gay Science*, New York: Dover Philosophical Classics

O'Gorman F., (2016), *Worrying: A Literary and Cultural History*, Reprint edition, London: Bloomsbury Academic

Ovide S., (2011), Warren Buffett on ethics: 'We can't afford to lose reputation', *Wall Street Journal*, 31 March, https://blogs.wsj.com/deals/2011/03/31/warren-buffett-on-ethics-we-cant-afford-to-lose-reputation

Patterson C.H., & Watkins E.C., (1996), *Theories of Psychotherapy*, New York: HarperCollins College Publishers

Payne W., (1985), *The Study of Emotion*, Ann Arbor MI: UMI

Pfeffer J., (2015), *Leadership BS: Fixing Workplaces and Careers One Truth at a Time*, New York: Harper Business

Porras J., Emery S., & Thompson M., (2007), *Success Built to Last: Creating a Life that Matters*, Reprint edition, Harlow: Plume

Ralston S., (2011), *John Dewey's Great Debates Reconstructed*, Charlotte NC: Information Age Publishing

Rank O., (2011), *Psychology and the Soul: A Study of the Origin, Conceptual Evolution, and Nature of the Soul*, Eastford CT: Martino Fine Books

Ratcliffe, M., (2008), *Feelings of Being: Phenomenology, Psychiatry and the Sense of Reality*, Oxford, UK: Oxford University Press

Ray A., (2017), *Mindfulness: Living in the Moment, Living in the Breath*, 3rd edition, New Brunswick: Inner Light Publishers

Reker G.T., (1996), Personal meaning in life and psychosocial adaptation in the later years, in P.T.P. Wong (Ed.), *The Human Quest for Meaning: Theories, Research and Applications*, Routledge

Reiss, S., (2000), *Who am I?: The 16 Basic Desires that Motivate our Behaviour and Define our Personality*, New York: Jeremy P. Tarcher/Putnam

Richard R.I., (1982), *Dialogue with C.G. Jung* (Dialogues in Contemporary Psychology Series), Santa Barbara: Praeger Publishers Inc

Richardson T., (2015), *The Responsible Leader*, London: Kogan Page

Salovey P., Brackett M.A., & Mayer J. (2004), *Key Readings on the Mayer and Salovey Model*, Portchester NY: National Professional Resources Inc

Sandling J., (2015), *Leading with Style: The Comprehensive Guide to Leadership Styles*, CreateSpace Independent Publishing

Sartre, J.P. (1966), *Being and Nothingness: An Essay on Phenomenological Ontology*, Tr. Hazel E. Barnes. New York: Washington Square Press, Inc.

Sartre J.P. (2000), *Words*, London: Penguin Classics

Schein E., (1992), *Organizational Culture and Leadership*, San Francisco: Jossey-Bass

Siddiqui F., (2017), *The Coveted Leader: 5 Pillars of Transformative Leadership*, Cupiditas

Spinelli E., (2007), *Practising Existential Psychotherapy: The Relational World*, London: Sage

Spinelli E., (2005), *The Interpreted World: An Introduction to Phenomenological Psychology*, London: Sage

Spurgeon C.H., (2018), *Words of Counsel (updated and annotated): For All Leaders, Teachers and Evangelists*, New Jersey: Aneko Press

Strasser F., & Strasser A., (1997), *Existential Time Limited Therapy*, London: Wiley

Thorndike E.L., (1920), Intelligence and its use, *Harpers Magazine*, 140, 227–235

Tillich P., (1952), *The Courage to Be*, New Haven CT: Yale University Press

Trilling L., (1972), *Sincerity and Authenticity*, Cambridge MA: Harvard University Press

Van Deurzen E., (1997), *Everyday Mysteries: Existential Dimensions of Psychotherapy*, London: Routledge

Van Deurzen-Smith E., (1984), Existential therapy, in W. Dryden (ed.), *Individual Therapy in Britain*, London: Harper & Row

Van Deurzen E., & Hanaway M. eds., (2012), *Existential Perspectives in Coaching*, London: Routledge

Van Dusen W., (1957), The theory and practice of existential analysis, *American Journal of Psychotherapy*, 11, 310–322

Villiers de l'Isle-Adam A., (2000), *Tomorrow's Eve*, Champaign IL: University of Illinois Press

Visser W., (2008), CSR in developing countries, in A. Crane, D. Matten, A. McWilliams, J. Moon, and D.S. Siegel (eds.), *The Oxford Handbook of Corporate Responsibility*, Oxford: Oxford University Press

Weber M., (1968), *On Charisma and Institution Building*, Chicago: University of Chicago Press

Weick K.E., (1995), *Sensemaking in Organizations*, London: Sage Publications

Yalom I., (1980), *Existential Psychotherapy*, New York: Basic Books

Index

Note: Page references in italic or bold type refer to figures or tables, respectively.

absurdity 2, 8–9, 11, 14, 18, 24
accountability 36–7, 45, 105
achievement(s) 34, 39, 83, **99**, 116
action(s): authentic 19, 73, 88; autonomous 64; as commitment 16; delegation of 69; doctrine of 14; embodied 6; free 29; inauthentic 75; leaderless 25; of leaders 31, 43, 44, 45, 49, 62, 75, 83, 87, 95, 103; meaningful 36; responsibility for 21, 40, 49, 61, 74, 105; styles of 90; underlying desires and values 77, 82, 96, 116
action patterns 10, 11, 16–17, 78–81
action plans 27
activism, global 38
adaptability **98**
affiliation 94, 97
aloneness 3, 11, 23, 40, 50
alternative dispute resolution (ADR) 5
analysis *see* psychoanalysis; psychotherapy
anxiety 5, 9–10, 11, 27, 104, 105; and the existential leader 60–4, 69; caused by freedom 64; existential 10, 11, 27; questions about 63
appreciation 94, 97
archetypal psychological types 90
Arendt, Hannah 21
atheism 20
authenticity 5, 7, 10, 11, 18–21, **98**, 105, 112, 113; and action 19, 73, 88; components of 73; and the existential leader 45, 54, 73–6; in listening 91; questions about 75; relational framework of 19, 73; *see also* inauthenticity

autonomy 61, 66, 67, 80, 94, 97, 107, 111
awareness 5, 6, 19, 32; and authenticity 73; of challenges 114; of death 12, 17, 41; emotional 39; existential 48, 62, 63, 85; of the needs of others 55, 73, 96, 119; organizational **99**; social **99**; of time and temporality 69–70; *see also* self-awareness

bad faith 1, 19, 21
Beauvoir, Simone de 1, 64
Becker, E. 17
being 1, 3, 5, 8, 14, 19, 21, 24, 45, 70, 85, 105, 114; potentiality for 14; reason for 114; ways of 42, 45, 46, 49, 57, 103, 114, 118
being-in-leadership-towards-others 118
being-in-the-world 12, 14, 46, 52
being-in-the-workplace 101
being towards the end 9, 10
beliefs 10–11, 14, 41, 46, 47, 60, 74, 76–8; existential 48; sedimented 10–11, 16–17, 78–81; shared 52
belonging 23, 52, 63, 90, 97, 103, 108, 109, 111
Bennis, Warren 25, 43
Berlin, I. 16
Binswanger, Ludwig 3
Blake, R.R. 33
Blake, William 12
bodily-kinesthetic intelligence 86
Boss, Medard 3
bracketing 2, 6, 61, 93
Brentano, Franz 12
Brexit 36, 37, 88
Brown, John Seely 83

burn out 46
business world: action patterns in 78–81; anxiety in 60–4; authenticity in 73–6; existential dimensions in *102*; freedom and responsibility in 64–9; leadership in 120; meaning in 82–4; philosophy in 49; psychology in 48–9; relatedness in 52–5; sedimented beliefs in 78–81; and time/temporality 69–72; uncertainty in 55–9; values in 78–81; *see also* existential leaders; leaders

Camus, Albert 8, 14; *L'Etranger* 11; *The Myth of Sisyphus* 14
Cartesian analysis 6
CEOs (chairmen), personality traits of 113–14
certainty: desire for 9, 105; false 58, 59, 60, 70, 114; illusion of 57, 60; lack of 5, 9, 55, 56, 58; need for 26, 72, 75; questioning 63; seeking 9, 56, 61, 72; threats to 61; *see also* uncertainty
Cerulo, Karen 9
change catalyst **100**
chaos, order in 114
Chesterton, G.K. 21
choice(s): cost of 114, 118; facticity and 14–16; freedom and 14–16; personal 1, 10–11, 61, 67, 74; responsibility for 2, 3, 11, 20, 108, 110; significance of 49
Christian beliefs 2, 20
clarity 87
collaboration 34, 41, **100**, 102
commitment 16, 19, 31, 32, 43, 50, 62, 63, 70, 73, 97, 116
communication: emotions in 97; interpersonal 55; and leadership 28, 42, 48, 49, 88, 106; nonverbal 86; stemming from five concerns 94; styles of 49, 90; *see also* listening
compassion 45, 54, 90
conflict management 49, 68, 97, **100**
consciousness 6, 16, 92, 94, 115
consistency 30, 87
consultancy 4, 48, 49
Cooper, David 4, 76
coping strategies 10, 90, 95, 102, 108
cosmic smarts 87
Cox, Gary 1
creativity 36, 58, 59, 62, 66, 67, 68, 77, 80, 89, 91, 101, 114, 118

Daseinsanalysis 3
das Man 21
death 27, 40, 41, 50, 56, 115; fear of 8, 50, 70; 'mini deaths' 17, 27, 70, 71; symbolic 17, 50; as wake-up call 70–1
Derrida, Jacques 7
dimensions, existential *see* existential dimensions
disappointment 113
disempowerment 61, 63, 65, 96, 118; *see also* empowerment
diversity 36, 40, 55
Drucker, Peter 25

ecological considerations 41
Eigenwelt 23, *78*, 96, **98**, **99**, **100**, 101, 110, 120
Emotional Intelligence (EI) 38–40, 43–4, 76–7, 87, 97; domains and competences linked to existential issues **98–100**
emotions 10, 11–13; listening for 94–5; negative 96; using 95–7, 101; and values 94–5
empathy 32, 39, 41, 92, **99**
employees: attitudes toward regulation and accountability 36–7; CEO or chairman 113–14; emotions of 94; needs of 48–51; operational managers 104–12; participation of 36; recruitment and retention of 37, 48; recruitment of 83, 90; retired 114–17; role of 94; senior leader/managers 112–13
empowerment 25, 30, 62, 64, 65, 79, 95, 118; *see also* disempowerment
engagement 19, 48, 50, 73, 77, 79, 112
Erickson, R.J. 20, 74
ethical issues 38, 41
existential analysis 3, 76–7, 82
existential dimensions 21–3, *22*, 24; in organizations *102*; physical (*Umwelt*) 22–3, *78*, **98**, **99**, **100**, 103, 109, 120; psychological (*Eigenwelt*) 23, *78*, **98**, **99**, **100**, 101, 103, 110, 120; social (*Mitwelt*) 23, *78*, **98**, **99**, **100**, 101, 103, 109–10, 120; spiritual (*(U)berwelt*) 23–4, *78*, **99**, **100**, 103, 111, 120; using 101–3
existential intelligence 85, 86–7
existentialism 7, 19, 47, 120; core issues 10–11, 68; defined 1–2; and emotion 12; emotional intelligence linked to

issues of **98–100**; and existential thought 5; and freedom 14; *see also* existential dimensions; existential intelligence; existential leaders; existential leadership

existential leaders: acceptance of responsibility 58, 62, 64–9; as authentic 45, 54, 73–6; becoming and remaining 120; beliefs of 47; delegation of power by 61–2; embodied values of 45, 47; knowing when to use structure and when not 120; on meaning 82–4; questions asked by 54–5, 58, 63, 68–9, 72, 75, 81, 83–4; reaction to anxiety 60–4, 69; reaction to uncertainty 57–60; as reflective and self-questioning 54; reliance on others 52, 55; response to freedom 64–9; response to human needs 48–9; response to time and temporality 69–72; on values 76–81; *see also* existential leadership; existential leadership skills

existential leadership: the CEO, MD, Chairman 113–14; focus on existential themes 40, 48; as leadership style 28; newly promoted operational manager/ team leader 104–12; as responsible leadership 45; the retired/non-exec 114–17; senior leader/manager seeking directorship 112–13; understanding of 1, 118–19; *see also* existential leadership skills

existential leadership skills 85; listening 88–95; types of intelligence 85–8; using emotions 95–7, 101; using existential dimensions 101–3

Existential Motivational Analysis (EMotiAn) 77, 82

existential-phenomenological theory 16

Existenzphilosophie 1; *see also* existentialism

extraversion 90

facticity 10, 11, 14–16
feedback 43, 44, 58, 60, 63, 66, 73, 74, 75, 89, **100**, 105
flexibility 67, 76, **98**
followers 119; coping strategies of 95; and leadership 25–6
Foucault, Michel 4
Frankl, Viktor 3–4, 14, 82; *see also* existential analysis

freedom 4, 5, 10, 11, 14–16, 20, 26, 40, 50, 107, 112; absolute 20; of choice 4, 45; enjoyed by leaders 64–5; existential 26; existentialist 14; positive 16; questions about 68–9; and responsibility 64–9; in retirement 116
Freud, Sigmun 17–18
Fromm, Erich 20
futures management techniques 9

Gardner, Howard 39, 85–6, 87
Gates, Bill 25
George, Bill 44
globalisation 37–8
God, death of 2, 15
Goleman, Daniel 38–40, 43
Grant, Adam 43
guidance 26, **100**
guilt 13, 26, 108; existential 10, 11

Harary, Charlie 67
Hartmann, Nicolai 7
Heidegger, Martin 1, 3, 7, 9, 12–13, 19, 20, 69, 73, 74; *Being and Time* 14, 21
Henry, Michel 7
herding animal morality 20
hermeneutics 3, 7
Hobbes, Thomas 14
hope 24, 45, 57, 102; death of 17, 70
human condition 2, 3, 11, 27, 85, 86, 87
Husserl, Edmund 2, 6–7, 12, 93

illusions: of certainty 57, 60; defined by circumstance 20; of individuality 20
immortality 17, 48
inauthenticity 5, 16, 19, 20, 21, 43, 44, 58, 64, 72, 73–4, 75, 81, 91, 104; *see also* authenticity
individualism 50
individuality 20; genuine 20; illusion of 20
influence 21, 25, 31, 74, 76, 77, 78, **100**, 105
information technology 35–6
Ingarden, Roman 7
initiative **99**
innovation 41, 67, 68, 85, 89, 90
insecurity 91
integrity 30, 41, 88, 102, 110
intelligence: bodily-kinesthetic 86; emotional 38–40, 43–4, 76–7, 87, 97; existential 85, 86–7; interpersonal 39, 40, 86; intra-personal 86; intrapersonal

39, 40; linguistic 86; logical-mathematical 86; multiple 39; musical 86; naturalist 86; social 39; spatial 86; spiritual 87
Intentional Change Model 46
intentionality 6, 12, 13, 45, 93–4
interdependence 40
interpersonal intelligence 39, 40, 86
intra-personal intelligence 86
introversion 90
Isle-Adam, Auguste de Villiers de l' 9
isolation 2, 5, 23, 50, 78, 96, 106, 108, 110, 112, 113, 114

Jaspers, Karl 1
Jung, Carl 90

Kierkegaard, Søren 2, 9, 10, 19, 20, 60, 73, 74
Kingsley Hall 4
knowledge: business 57, 59, 95, 113, 114; existential 5, 6, 8, 37, 49, 50, 63, 64, 72, 101, 105; global 38; partial 58; as power 18; scientific 3; self- 1, 20, 86; sharing 41

Lacan, Jacques 4
Laing, R.D. 4
Lao Tzu 31
leaderless resistance 25
leaders: authentic 43–4, 64, 73–6, 118; authoritative 29; autocratic 29; benevolent authoritative 28; charismatic 30–1; connective 40–3; consultative 29; coping strategies of 95; emotional intelligent 38–40; and the expectations of others 74; exploitive authoritative 28; insecure 91; as models 26–7; participative 29; people-oriented 34; quiet 31; resonant 45–7; responsible 45; and the search for meaning 26; servant 32, 46; task-oriented 33; transactional 29, 30; transformative 29–31, 95; types of 27–8; *see also* existential leaders; leadership
leadership: and action patterns 78–81; ambivalent relationship with 27; authentic 38, 41; collaborative 41; connective 38; defined 25; existential 40; exploratory 41; inspirational 41, **99**; negative styles 34; preferences 32–4; relational framework of 47; resonant 38; responsible 38; and the search for meaning 30; transactional 95; transformational 95; X and Y theory 32–3, 80; *see also* existential leadership; existential leadership skills; leaders
leadership theory 25–6
Levinas, Emmanuel 4, 7, 12
Levithan, David 9
life-world 6
linguistic intelligence 86
listening 88–94; active 91–3; effective 89; for expression of emotions 94–5
listening skills 90
Locke, John 14
logical-mathematical intelligence 86
logotherapy 3–4
loneliness 53, 54, 56, 96, 108, 116
loyalty 17, 67, 79, 87, 89

management styles 33, 80
management theory 80
Managerial Grid 33
Marcel, Gabriel 7
Marion, Jean-Luc 7
Maxwell, John 25
May, Paul 3
May, Rollo 3, 111
McGregor, Douglas 32
meaning 5, 10, 11, 14, 40, 41, 48, 49, 50, 82–4; making of 83; need for 76–7; questions about 83–4
meaninglessness 2, 3, 5, 14, 111
Mengel, Thomas 76–7
Menkes, Justin 113–14
Merleau-Ponty, Maurice 3, 4, 7, 12
mindfulness 44, 45, 92
mine-ness 20
mirroring 7
Mitwelt 23, 78, 96, **98**, **99**, **100**, 101, 109–10, 120
morality 11, 16, 20
mortality 3, 11, 12, 22, 24, 116; and time 10, 17–18
motivation 11, 20, 31, 39, 74, 75, 77, 115; self-40
motivational psychotherapy 82
motivational skill 31
motivational theory 82
Mouton, S. 33
musical intelligence 86
Myers-Briggs test 90

National Listening Association 91

naturalist intelligence 86
neuroscience 39
neurosis 17
New School of Psychotherapy and Counseling (NSPC) 4
Nichols, Ralph 91
Nietzsche, Friedrich 2, 19, 20, 73, 74; *The Gay Science* 15; *Thus Spoke Zarathustra* 15
noema and noesis 6, 93–4

ontology 9, 69, 85, 107
open-mindedness 92
optimism **99**; realistic 114
optimistic bias 9
order in chaos 114
organisational awareness **99**

paradox 3, 5, 6, 8, 22, 44, 61, 67, 72, 74, 76, 87, 101; in Steve's example 107–111; in worldview *107*
parenthood 65
participation 29, 36, 41
passion 2, 8–9, 11, 18, 20, 30, 67–8, 72, 80, 83, 101
Payne, Wayne 39
Pfeffer, Jeff 43
phantom cell structure 25
phenomenology 2–3, 5–7, 12, 90, 93
Philadelphia Association 4
philosophy: and business 48, 49; existential 2, 5, 19, 73, 120; existential-phenomenological 3; Greek 18; western 1, 2; *see also* existentialism; phenomenology
Positive Organisational Behavior (POB) 75
power: appetite for 27; attainment of 23, 44; collective 53; delegation of 61–2; of followers 27, 53; knowledge as 18; of leaders 27, 29, 30, 38, 41, 44, 53, 64, 66, 90, 105; leader's relationship with 61; limitations on 62, 65; of parents 65; physical 109; of sedimented beliefs 16–17; sharing 32, 61–2, 64, 68, 74; surrender of 116; transfer of 116; *see also* disempowerment; empowerment
power dynamics 49
powerlessness 61
processing, unbiased 19, 73
psychoanalysis 3, 18; existential 3, 76–7, 82; *see also* psychotherapy

psychology 2, 39; and business 48–9
psychometrics 90
psychosis 17
psychotherapy 3, 4; motivational 82; time limited 4; *see also* psychoanalysis
purpose 5, 8, 9, 14, 16, 24, 26, 29, 30, 36, 39, 41, 44, 50, 67–8, 77, 88, 96, 114

questions: about anxiety 63; about authenticity 75; about freedom 68–9; about leaders 118; about meaning 83–4; about relatedness 54; about responsibility 69; about time and temporality 72; about uncertainty 58, 63; about values 81; for an existential leader to ask 54–5, 58, 63, 68–9, 72, 75, 81, 83–4; for senior leaders/managers to ask 113

Rank, Otto 3, 17
Ratcliffe, M. 13
Ray, Amit 60
recruitment 37, 48, 83, 90
Reed, Jamie 104
regulation 36–7
Reiss, Steven 77, 82
Reiss Motivational Profile (RMP) 77, 82
relatedness 5, 7–8, 9, 45, 52–5, 88; questions about 54
relational components 19
relationship building **100**
religion 20
resilience 44; emotional 97, 101
respect 92
responsibility 5, 10, 11, 14–16, 26, 45, 105, 112; and freedom 64–9; questions about 69; in retirement 116; shared 64
retention 37, 48
retirement 114–17
Richadson, Tim 45
Ricoeur, Paul 7, 12
risk assessment 57
risk management 59
risk taking 31, 69, 74, 108
risks: creative 37, 66, 67; of leadership 27, 53, 59, 63, 65
Rousseau, Jean Jacques 14

sacrifice syndrome 46
Sartre, Jean-Paul 1, 3, 4, 7, 12, 14, 15, 19, 21, 64, 73
Schein, Edgar 76

Scheler, Max 7, 12
Schütz, Alfred 7
sedimented beliefs 10–11, 16–17, 78–81
self-acceptance 7
self-affirmation 23
self-assessment **98**
self-awareness 7, 39, 40, 43, 44, 45, 73, 74, 76, **98**; *see also* awareness
self-concept 8, 43, 73, 97, 108
self-confidence 27, **98**, 105
self-constructs 17
self-control **98**
self-criticism 43, 73, 119
self-delusion 9, 114
self-esteem 48, 65, 66, 68, 90, 105, 109, 110, 112, 114
self-identity 70, 114, 115
self-importance 23
self-knowledge 1, 20
self-management **98**
self-reflection 43, 73, 118, 119, 120
self-regulation 39
sense-making 76
service **99**
sincerity 19; *see also* authenticity
social awareness **99**
social skills 39, 85
Socrates 1, 74
Solomon, Robert 12
Sources of Meaning Profile (SOMP) 77, 82
spatial intelligence 86
specialness 18, 26
Spinelli, Ernesto 4, 9, 17
spiritual intelligence 87–8
status 70, 71, 77, 81, 94, 97, 102
Stein, Edith 7
Strasser, Freddie 4, 13
strength(s) 62, 63, 74, 87; emotional 97; of intelligences 86; in leaders 87; personal 23; physical 109, 110; and weaknesses 19, 23, 39, 46, 48, 73, 75, 97
stress management 49, 62
Stuart Mill, John 14
subservience to purpose 114
suffering 4, 70, 74, 80

team work 48–9, 68, **100**

temporality 5, 41, 47, 48, 49, 61, 114; questions about 72; and time 69–72; *see also* time
theology 2
Thompson, Mark 67
thrownness 5, 15, 61, 65, 111, 120
Thucydides 14
time 5, 10, 11, 47, 48, 114; and mortality 17–18; questions about 72; and temporality 69–72; *see also* temporality
transactional skills 90
transparency **98**
Trump, Donald J. 38, 88

Überwelt 23–4, *78*, 96, **99**, **100**, 111, 120
Umwelt 22–3, *78*, 96, **98**, **99**, **100**, 109, 120
uncertainty 88, 105–6, 113; acknowledging 38; anxiety of 16, 56, 57, 60; and authenticity 19, 64, 104; avoiding 9, 26, 56, 105; and 'being' 5; defense/guarding against 17, 26, 50, 59, 75, 91; dread of 48; economic 35; of the employee 105–6, 113, 114; of existence 8–9, 10, 11, 22, 27, 37–8, 96; existential 27, 59, 60, 114; and the existential leader 45, 55–9, 62; power over 27; questions about 58, 63, 72; response to 45; and responsibility 16; temporal 105; threat of 88

values 5, 10, 10–11, 14, 16–17, 41, 45, 46, 47, 60, 62, 76–81; basic 77; and action patterns 11; and emotions 94–5; importance of 78; motivational 77, *78*; questions about 81; shared 49
van Deurzen, Emmy 4, 9
virtue(s), religious 20
vision statement 57, 81
Voegelin, Eric 7

Weber, Max 30
Weick, Karl 76
well-being 32, 39, 74
Wittgenstein, Ludwig 4
work: and the millennial workforce 67; as place to find meaning 50, 69–70
worldview 10–11; paradoxes in *107*
worry 9, 12, 93

Yalom, Irvin D. 5, 18, 26